MY EXCELLENCY

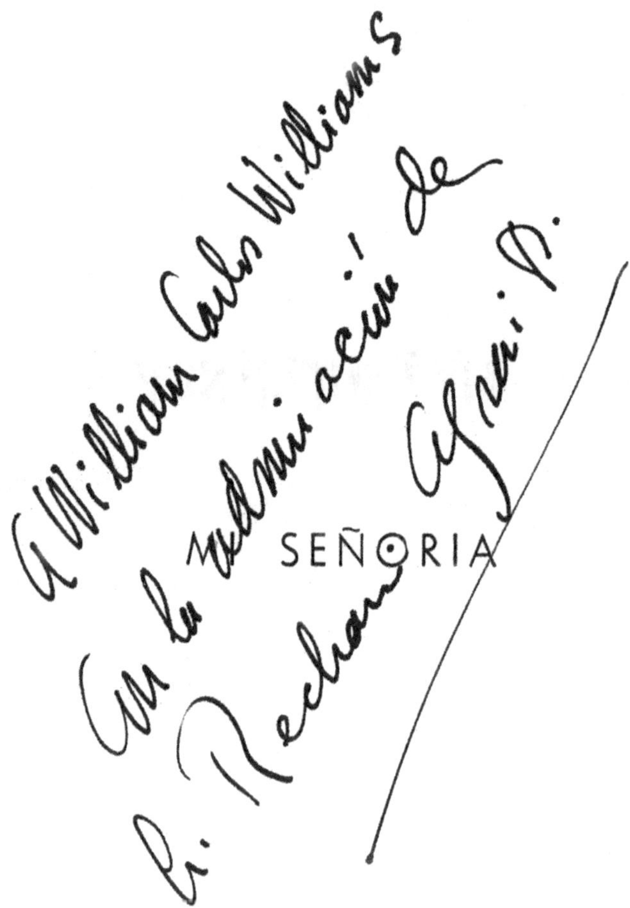

Luis Rechani Agrait's inscription to William Carlos Williams in his gifted 1940 edition of *Mi señoría*. Courtesy of Beinecke Rare Book and Manuscript Library, Yale University.

MY EXCELLENCY

COMEDY IN THREE ACTS

LUIS RECHANI AGRAIT

TRANSLATED FROM THE SPANISH BY
William Carlos Williams

EDITED AND WITH AN INTRODUCTION BY
Jonathan Cohen

FOREWORD BY
Julio Marzán

AFTERWORD BY
José Luis Ramos Escobar

SWAN ISLE PRESS
CHICAGO

Swan Isle Press, Chicago 60611

First Edition

29 28 27 26 25   1 2 3 4 5

ISBN: 978-1-961056-11-4 (paper)
ISBN: 978-1-961056-16-9 (ebook)

First published by Puerto Rico Ilustrado in 1940 as *Mi señoría* by Luis Rechani Agrait.

Cover image: Carlos Rechani Agrait as Buenaventura Padilla in the original production of *Mi señoría*. Photograph from Luis Rechani Agrait, *Mi señoría* (Puerto Rico Ilustrado, 1940).

Library of Congress Cataloging-in-Publication Data

Names: Rechani Agrait, Luis author | Williams, William Carlos, 1883-1963 translator | Cohen, Jonathan, 1949 May 4- editor writer of introduction Marzán, Julio, 1946- writer of foreword | Ramos Escobar, José Luis writer of afterword
Title: My Excellency : Comedy in Three Acts / Luis Rechani Agrait; translated from the Spanish by William Carlos Williams ; edited and with an introduction by Jonathan Cohen; foreword by Julio Marzán; afterword by José Luis Ramos Escobar.
Other titles: *Mi señoría*. Spanish
Identifiers: LCCN 2025037377 (print) | LCCN 2025037378 (ebook) | ISBN 9781961056114 paperback | ISBN 9781961056169 epub
Subjects: LCGFT: Comedy plays | Drama
Classification: LCC PQ7439.R42 M513 2025 (print) | LCC PQ7439.R42 (ebook)
LC record available at https://lccn.loc.gov/2025037377
LC ebook record available at https://lccn.loc.gov/2025037378

Swan Isle Press gratefully acknowledges that this book has been made possible, in part, with the generous support of grants and funding from the following:

Illinois ARTS Council ILLINOIS ARTS COUNCIL AGENCY
EUROPE BAY GIVING TRUST
OTHER KIND DONORS

This paper meets the requirements of ANSI/NISO Z39.48-1992 (Permanence of Paper).

CONTENTS

Illustrations *vii*

Foreword: Another Expression of the Spanish American Roots of William Carlos Williams, Julio Marzán *ix*

Introduction: Recovering Williams's Translation Debuting Rechani Agrait in the American Idiom, Jonathan Cohen *xi*

My Excellency

Characters | Time and Place 2

First Act 5

Second Act *41*

Third Act Synopsis *77*

Acto Tercero *81*

Afterword: Luis Rechani Agrait and Modern Puerto Rican Drama, José Luis Ramos Escobar *109*

Lecture: An Informal Discussion of Poetic Form, William Carlos Williams *113*

Acknowledgments *119*

Biographies *121*

ILLUSTRATIONS

Luis Rechani Agrait's inscription to William Carlos Williams *ii*

Juan, Mariana, Buenaventura Padilla, Peñita, and Concepción *4*

Juan, Concepción, and Buenaventura Padilla *40*

Buenaventura Padilla and Peñita *76*

Drawing of the set for the third act by Pedro Luis Tosado *80*

Ticket for the premiere of *Mi señoría* *108*

William Carlos Williams's typed lecture notes *112*

Luis Rechani Agrait as a boy with his father and mother *120*

FOREWORD

Another Expression of the Spanish American Roots of William Carlos Williams

The First Inter-American Writers' Conference, to which Williams was invited to speak in 1941, showcased Puerto Rico's distinct cultural vitality despite four decades of the United States' efforts to impose Anglo-Protestant culture and the English language. This resistance had produced a generation of writers and intellectuals who celebrated the island's Hispanic heritage and Hispanist scholars who achieved renown from Spain to Latin America. Williams landed in this cultural battleground as the much respected, in poet Muna Lee's words, "prodigal son."

During his visit, the dreamed Puerto Rico evoked by Williams's mother, Elena, in her reminiscences became tangible, and he discovered the convergence of his "Spanish" literary background with distinctly Caribbean and Puerto Rican legacies. The experience was less a culture shock than a confirmation, as Williams had already had contact with that Puerto Rico on the mainland after the Puerto Rican translator and critic Angel Flores published Williams's story collection *The Knife of the Times* under his imprint Dragon Press.

Still, Williams could not have anticipated his visit's influence on his work, which was most notably impacted by the poetry and Caribbean vision of Luis Palés Matos. After his visit, Williams translated Palés's "Preludio en Boricua" ("Prelude in Boricua") and even imitated Palés in some poems. The poet's work explained much about Elena, inspiring a controlling metaphor that fed Williams's determination to write his "personal record" of his mother, *Yes, Mrs. Williams*. Similarly, as Williams suggested years later, Palés's major book, *Tuntún de pasa y grifería* (Tom-Tom of Kinky Hair and Things Black), provided the "scheme" for him to start *Paterson,* as well as influencing Williams's Caribbean consciousness in writing the play *Tituba's Children.*

I wrote *The Spanish American Roots of William Carlos Williams* unaware that Williams had translated the three-act comedy *Mi señoría* by Luis Rechani Agrait, a member of the aforementioned distinguished island generation. Rechani's farcical play, set in a fictitious country, satirizes Puerto Rican politics with an idealistic party leader who is betrayed by followers vulnerable to the hamartia of materialism. When I read the play, I was unable to divorce my knowing that if Williams translated *Mi señoría,* then in it he had found something of himself.

One kindred feature between Williams and Rechani's drama is its language play, both in the colorful island dialogue and in the protagonist Buenaventura Padilla's malapropisms. Williams would often jot down how his mother said things in an "island" way, at times misusing English, which her son heard as spontaneous poetry. Another similar theme is Buenaventura's idealism, which causes him to deny reality at the cost of his sanity. This criollo psyche, also satirized by Palés Matos, coincides with Williams's critique of his mother's escapism and her romanticization of an island to which she would never return.

Unfortunately, Williams's translation is missing *Mi señoría*'s third act, whether lost or unfinished. However, his translated two acts valuably demonstrate the connection Williams identified between the younger playwright's baroque wit and his own Spanish-rooted lineage, what he ambiguously referred to (always in quotation marks) as his "line." In recovering Williams's translation of *Mi señoría,* Jonathan Cohen offers readers a significant gift, as he has done before with translations of previously unknown works. Thanks to this recovery, we now have more of Williams, and with this book we can further appreciate the undeniable "Carlos" (versus "Bill") in him and his canon.

Julio Marzán
New York, 2025

INTRODUCTION

Recovering Williams's Translation Debuting Rechani Agrait in the American Idiom

William Carlos Williams's engagement with Puerto Rico—his mother's fabled homeland, island of the Carlos in him—was never more intense than in 1941, when he made his first visit there at the age of fifty-seven. He visited in April, when the island's weather is perfect, warm with bright sun, before the rains of summer. He had been invited to speak at an international writers' conference sponsored by the University of Puerto Rico just outside San Juan, the First Inter-American Writers' Conference. It was a ten-day affair with a full program of lectures, tours, roundtable discussions, and social events. Williams, who had brought his wife, Florence ("Floss"), stayed for a week. They were put up with other VIP delegates at the Condado Vanderbilt Hotel, the first luxury hotel to open in Puerto Rico, overlooking the ocean. He enjoyed tremendously the beauty of the island's tropical nature, the "flowers, birds . . . , mango trees, palms with coconuts high up, hibiscus," which he described in a letter to his son William Eric. He also enjoyed the attention he received as a speaker at the conference. His attendance there was news. *El Mundo*, San Juan's major newspaper, published a front-page photograph of him standing next to another speaker, Jorge Mañach of Cuba, with the header "Distinguished Writers Who Are Visiting Us." Other distinguished writers chosen as conference delegates had traveled to Puerto Rico from throughout Latin America and from the United States, including Archibald MacLeish. One of the principal organizers of the conference was the US-born poet Muna Lee, then resident of Puerto Rico and the premier translator of Latin American poets into English during the first half of the twentieth century, whom Williams held in high regard (see my biography of her in *A Pan-American Life*). Williams's lecture was titled "An Informal Discussion of Poetic Form" (reproduced at the end of this volume), and it was very well received. In keeping with his poetics, he stressed the need to incorporate into poetry the American vernacular, the language as actually spoken. He stressed, too, that US poets could learn much from Spanish poetry, as he himself had in his formative years: "*What* influence can Spanish have on us who speak a derivative of English in North America? To shake us free for a reconsideration of the poetic line," he proclaimed. Moreover, he stated that the "four-stressed line" (octosyllabic meter) in Spanish Golden Age verse drama offered a model that could advance American theater—something Williams himself was doing at that very moment as a playwright.

Drama was center stage in Williams's creative life at the time. Before and after visiting Puerto Rico, he was at work on his three-act play *Trial Horse No. 1,* which ultimately became *Many Loves,* his most successful play (it ran for nearly a year in New York at the off-Broadway Living Theatre in 1959). Its verse passages do indeed echo early modern Spanish theater. Drama was a passion Williams had pursued since his youth as both an amateur actor and playwright. This aspect, however, has been little appreciated among readers of his work. Biographer Paul Mariani points out that Williams "thought first of becoming an actor and a dramatist before he opted for poetry," though it can be argued that "opting" for one art over the other is a false dichotomy. Drama informed Williams's poetics from the start of his career. Around 1914, he translated from Spanish Lope de Vega's Golden Age verse play *El Nuevo Mundo descubierto por Cristóbal Colón* (*The New World Discovered by Christopher Columbus*), an early apprenticeship in the technique that would help him attain his mature voice as a poet. While the translation has been lost, Williams's swift-moving baroque language in the American idiom was first demonstrated in his breakthrough book of modernist poems, *Al Que Quiere!* (1917). The concluding remarks of his talk in Puerto Rico emphasized his connection with the poetics of Lope's drama: "We have a problem before us in the United States to find a verse form that will be suitable for the theater. We know it can never be blank verse. It may very well be that in hints from the *romancero* [collection of old ballads] or at least Lope's shorter, swifter line, we will finally discover something more acceptable to our temperament, manner of thought, and speech."

Williams met several writers at the conference who greatly impressed him. Lee was among them, though she was no stranger to him. Early in her career as a poet (early in his too), she published her work in *Others*, of which he was an associate editor at the time. They first met in person in New York in 1919. Her translations of Latin American poets came to his attention in *Poetry*'s 1925 special issue *Spanish-American Number*, and later her Jorge Carrera Andrade translations amazed him ("I don't know when I have had so clear a pleasure," he'd tell her in 1942). Williams also engaged with the poet Luis Palés Matos at the conference, who made a strong impression. Palés gave Williams a copy of his book of poems *Tuntún de pasa y grifería* (Tom-Tom of Kinky Hair and Things Black), which had come out four years before. Its prefatory poem "Preludio en Boricua," with its use of local talk in an Afro-Antillean voice, appealed to Williams. He was inspired to translate this poem ("plenty tough to render into American," he told Lee) and to publish his translation "Prelude in Boricua" the following year—*Boricua* meaning Puerto Rican Spanish, deriving from the aboriginal name of the island.

It was also at the conference that Williams met the Puerto Rican journalist and playwright Luis Rechani Agrait, about twenty years his junior and a rising star in the world of Puerto Rican theater. They had a lot in common, both aesthetically and politically. Rechani aimed to write plays native to Puerto Rico in theme and language, and Williams aimed for a similar localism in his own work. Rechani gave him an autographed copy of his three-act play *Mi señoría*, which had debuted the previous fall and was published later in the year. It was Rechani's first play to be staged and receive critical attention. His inscription to Williams states: "A William Carlos Williams / Con la admiración de / L. Rechani Agrait" (To William Carlos Williams / With the admiration of / L. Rechani Agrait). The play, now considered a classic in Puerto Rican theater, is a brilliant political farce. Once home and able to read it, most likely with the help of his mother who was living with him and his family, Williams could not resist the urge to translate the play. For him it became *My Excellency*.

Lee called this translation project "extremely important news" in the newspaper *Puerto Rico World Journal*—that "[Williams] will translate and submit to a U.S. producer Rechani Agrait's *Mi señoría*." In her regular column, she quoted from a letter Williams had written to her in early May, soon after the conference: "The revolution in my sensual filing-cabinet has been so complete that I remain like a man between two worlds, the old with all the geography-book pictures of the West Indies in it and the thrilling new in which all of you at the University [of Puerto Rico] appear. I hardly know which is real and which the illusion but it's getting clearer day by day. We had to be home again before we could realize how very fortunate we had been, the whole schedule of it right out of a dream." He went on to say: "I was also delighted with Rechani Agrait. Come what may I'll do his play into good American for him and submit it to someone here before another year is out.... Time is the thing—I am swamped with the minute affairs of my life until I think that everything is already over and ended. The days immediately following my return were diabolic, day and night, two babies and people in the office like ants—more or less." Looking back on his visit, he told Lee, "I think I have never enjoyed a more satisfying journey from home. I'll be digesting my experiences there in Puerto Rico for years to come."

Rechani must have been very excited to know that Williams desired to translate him. A production of his play in English on the mainland had the potential to boost his career as a playwright significantly. His path to this point had been remarkable. Born in 1902 in the town of Aguas Buenas, south of San Juan, Rechani was known as a journalist, poet, and short-story writer when *Mi señoría* was produced in 1940 at the University of Puerto Rico's theater. The play combined his diverse writing background and long concern with social and historical issues. He had spent several prior years living in the United States while attending first Harvard and then the University of Richmond. After he returned to Puerto Rico, he worked for

El Mundo as editor in chief. Public matters were the primary focus of his attention. He left the paper after a couple of years to work in the Department of Public Instruction as assistant to the commissioner. During this period he published two books for children: a reader, *Páginas de color de rosa* (1928; Rose-Colored Pages), and a book of poems with fellow poet Rafael Rivera Otero, *Una nube en el viento* (1929; A Cloud in the Wind). In 1930 he returned to *El Mundo* and worked there over the next decade, during which he published several short stories, most appearing in the weekly magazine *Puerto Rico Ilustrado*, which was delivered as an insert in *El Mundo*.

Stimulated by the activity in Puerto Rican theater in the late 1930s, Rechani resumed writing drama, following his previous efforts, which had resulted in two unpublished comedies: "Contra la vida" (1926; Against Life) and "Tu mujer no te engaña" (1934; Your Wife Doesn't Cheat on You). He wrote *Mi señoría* in 1937. Three years later, he brought the play to the attention of a new theater company that had formed to produce experimental theater in search of a national identity, the first company on the island dedicated to a vital dramaturgy of genuine national character—like the poetry of the American idiom that Williams himself sought. Called the Sociedad Dramática Areyto (Areyto Dramatic Society) after the name given to the dramatic tribal dance of Puerto Rico's native people (Williams knew about the *areito* from translating Lope's *El Nuevo Mundo*), the company emphasized the need to create Puerto Rican characters, situations, and landscapes for the stage. *Mi señoría* fit the bill perfectly and Areyto produced it. The play, which was among the company's first productions, was an immediate success with audiences and critics alike. *El Mundo* called it "un triunfo definitivo" (a definite triumph) and "bello, ameno y penetrante" (beautiful, entertaining, and piercing). Radio news commentator Coronel Sicardo said the play "se nos impuso desde el momento mismo en que entró en acción la trama en aquel magnífico primer acto, que resulta un primor de técnica y gracia" (captivated us from the very moment in which the plot unfolded in that magnificent first act, which turns out to be a marvel of craft and farce).

Set in an "imaginary country" that resembles Puerto Rico during the Great Depression, with its very high unemployment and labor unrest, *Mi señoría* deals with the plight of an idealistic but naive man, Buenaventura Padilla, in a completely corrupt political system. The name Buenaventura literally means "good fortune" in Spanish, ironically here. After twenty years of fighting for social justice and for his Workers Party to gain control of the country, Buenaventura finally becomes president of the Chamber of Deputies, in effect the national leader, by resorting to the same unethical methods that his enemies had used successfully in past elections. Once in office, he tries to bring about a range of much-needed social reforms, but the uneducated and unscrupulous characters he appoints to government positions abuse their power and betray him. The play is successful as political satire largely because of Buenaventura's hilariously funny language, his grandiloquent style combined with stunning malapropisms and clownish errors in history and grammar. In his translation of the play, Williams's artistic skill with vernacular creates real dialogue, and the timing is controlled for maximum comic effect. The play's dialogue often resounds with the coarseness of language used by the working class, like the language of Williams's own patients and other Jersey locals he portrayed in his short stories throughout the 1930s. He knew this language well and could effectively create in his American idiom an accurate equivalent of the Spanish. At times he also mixes Spanish words in the dialogue for a dimension of Spanglish that resists domestication of the source text.

Rechani scholar Nilda González offers this assessment in her essay "Apuntes sobre el teatro de Luis Rechani Agrait" (Notes on the Theater of Luis Rechani Agrait) published by the Institute of Puerto Rican Culture:

> To think about Rechani's theater is to immediately recall the laughter provoked by his characters and the situations they create; it is to think of Buenaventura Padilla saying nonsense to his fellow party members. . . . [Rechani's comedies] provoke our laughter, that is true, but it is not a happy joyful laughter, but one that hides pain, anguish, pathos. Behind the apparent laughter of Rechani's theater there are several elements of a social, human, political nature, which should not

> be lost sight of. As an author, he looks at the reality around him, drawing inspiration from it and transforming it into something grotesque, ridiculous, that apparently makes no sense, but which hides sad, bitter truths. This bittersweet tone of laughter provoked by Rechani's theater is therefore the product of what each situation or character represents, and it is at the same time the awareness we have that what makes us laugh at a scene is what causes our suffering in real life.

Buenaventura's naivete and idealism lead him to political heights, then depths, in what is ultimately a sad end. In the intense national consciousness reflected in Buenaventura and his love of his people, the playwright's commitment to Areyto's mission is absolutely clear.

Why no scholar has ever addressed Williams's translation of this marvelous play is a mystery to me. The explanation may simply be that since it was never performed or published, it went unnoticed. Lack of any mention of it in his published correspondence also contributes to its apparent nonexistence. At the same time, since his translation work in general—all the poetry and fiction from Spanish, French, Greek, and Chinese—has largely been ignored by scholars, *My Excellency* has likely lost out from getting attention for this reason as well. Together with his own dramatic work in the late 1930s and early 1940s, the act of translation was good exercise in dramatic writing for Williams. Indeed, translating Rechani's play gave him the opportunity to practice "straight theater prose," as he described the script of *Many Loves*, "not poetic drama." In "The Outrage of *Many Loves*," Linda Wagner observes that the play's "spotlight on dialogue," rather than plot, resembles the compositional method of his "best short stories"—as seen in the stories in Williams's *Life Along the Passaic River* (1938). In 1941, playwriting had again become very important to him, with *Many Loves* a priority project. Later that year he put considerable effort into interesting producers to do the show, without any luck.

The typescript rendering of the first two acts of *My Excellency* is buried in Williams's papers in the University at Buffalo's Poetry Collection. That it looks essentially finished, with a title page and none of his typical elaborate edits throughout the script, leads me to conclude the third act was translated as well but is now lost. Maybe it will be found one day among his scattered papers across different libraries—a mystery in itself. Here, my synopsis of the missing act provides a summary of its dramatic action and the play's outcome, and the entire Spanish text follows it. One can only wonder if his translation, in part or in full, ever reached the eyes of a producer, as there is no apparent record of his efforts to promote Rechani.

A week after Williams returned from Puerto Rico to his home in New Jersey, a splashy front-page story about the writers' conference was published in *El Mundo*'s weekly magazine, *Puerto Rico Ilustrado,* which featured several pages with photographs of him and other delegates at the conference. Also included in the same issue of the magazine was a Spanish translation of his essay "The Fountain of Eternal Youth," from his 1925 collection *In the American Grain,* about Juan Ponce de León, the first governor of Puerto Rico. A photo of Williams sitting outside on a stone, looking left with an intense poet's gaze, accompanied the translation. In early May, *Puerto Rico Ilustrado* published an additional long feature article about him titled "Chispazo de [Flash of] William Carlos Williams." Muna Lee gave him this news in a letter and told him the author of the article "avowedly sees you as the Atlas bearing the entire burden of U.S. literature on your shoulders (one foot, of course, firmly planted in Puerto Rico)." Lee emphasized to Williams, "You may be sure that Puerto Rico will not forget you and has very evidently taken you to her heart as her prodigal son." Clearly, Puerto Rico had also found a place deep in his heart during his visit to the island. His translations of the drama, poetry, and fiction he received as gifts from its writers allowed him to explore in words and celebrate his Puerto Rican side, the Carlos in him. How pleased he would be to know that his performance of Rechani Agrait's *My Excellency* in the American idiom will at last be enjoyed on these pages here.

Jonathan Cohen
New York, 2025

MY EXCELLENCY

CHARACTERS

(In the order in which they speak)

TONIA, a supporter of Buenaventura

CONCEPCIÓN, another supporter, then a girlfriend of Don Ramón

MARIANA, another supporter

JUAN, the bodyguard and old friend of Buenaventura

BORRACHO,* another supporter

PEÑITA, another supporter, then opponent

TORTILLITA, another supporter

FIRST MAN, another supporter

SECOND MAN, another supporter

THIRD MAN, another supporter

BLIND MAN (later, Administrator of the Homes for the Aged), another supporter

BUGLER (later, Director of the Conservatory of Music), another supporter

CARMELA, the daughter of Buenaventura

JAIME, the secretary and protégé of Buenaventura

BUENAVENTURA PADILLA, candidate for president of the Chamber of Deputies, then president

GUARD, assigned to Buenaventura

COLMENERO, a journalist

---

*Drunk, in Spanish.

DON RAMÓN TORRES, a gangster multimillionaire and nemesis of Buenaventura

WOUNDED MAN, another supporter of Buenaventura

GEORGE, the son of Don Ramón

GANG LEADER, a thug who works for Don Ramón

TIRADO, a policeman

BELLBOY, at hotel where banquet honoring Buenaventura is held

(Women workers, men workers, gang members)

TIME AND PLACE

The present. An imaginary country, where evidently the president of the Chamber of Deputies exercises important government functions; surely otherwise Buenaventura Padilla had better have been president of the Council of Ministers, with the sole omission of the gavel and a phrase or two in the third act. The workers are encouraged to corrupt the language according to their own taste. And the director, as is customary, will change the action to suit their pleasure following the inclination of the characters.

Left to right: Juan (Walter Busó), Mariana (Delia Esther Quiñones), Buenaventura Padilla (Benjamín Morales), Peñita (Félix Antelo), and Concepción (Jennie Sosa). From the 1966 production of *Mi señoría* presented by the Institute of Puerto Rican Culture (Instituto de Cultura Puertorriqueña) at the Tapia Theater in San Juan, Puerto Rico. Photograph courtesy of the Institute of Puerto Rican Culture—General Archives of Puerto Rico.

First Act

Before the curtain goes up shouts are heard, trumpet blasts, tramping and running, vivas for the Workers Party and for Buenaventura Padilla, and cries of "We will win this election." A quick curtain, the scene represents a small office (or is it merely a living room of certain pretensions?) of the Labor Party Club, on the second floor, dawn of Election Day. Everything denotes simplicity and extreme poverty. Fastened to the dark and dirty walls, photos of labor workers clipped from reviews. Perhaps a placard, bearing the legend VOTE THIS WAY and the insignia of the party (a pair of crossed brooms) marked with a cross to show how it should be done. Perhaps someone has scrawled on the wall, letter by letter, WE WANT SOCIAL JUSTICE. Several chairs, one of them broken down, crammed with paper-covered books and old periodicals. At the left, a window overlooking the street. Near it a bench and beside it a rough table with an old typewriter. At the right, a door which opens into other rooms, to the lower floor, and the street in the rear. At the back, center, a door which opens on a passageway, through which turning to the left and descending a stair, one comes to the main entrance of the building, while turning to the right one arrives at the room where Buenaventura Padilla directs the electoral campaign of his party. It is a pity that though the door at the back is open at the moment, you can see only the hallway and not Buenaventura Padilla, seated at his desk, giving orders, surrounded by eager henchmen. We have to content ourselves with witnessing those of his friends and helpers who, coming or leaving, cross hurriedly through. But one can hear, sometimes clear, sometimes confused, according to the excitement of the moment, the noise of his followers and now and again pointlessly a trumpet blast, like those heard formerly. Likewise we shall not be able to see the main entrance to the building, before which a lively crowd has stationed itself all through the night, occasionally obstructing traffic which has captured the entire interest of CONCEP-

CIÓN and TONIA, who are looking out of the window at the left. Concepción, a timid and modest young girl, is sitting on a bench with her arms on the windowsill, and Tonia, a plain sort of woman, standing behind her. The only other person at present in the room is JUAN, an old laborer of about fifty years of age, who believes himself a wild man but who in reality is a good-natured enough fellow. Juan, who is tired and annoyed, is about to remove the table to some other part of the room, but can't make up his mind where. The FIRST MAN enters like a streak of lightning through the door at the right and exits again at the back right. Evidently he is bringing a message for Buenaventura Padilla, and it seems that he has also received instructions from him, for in a moment he returns on the run at the back, right, with TORTILLITA, and both leave by the door right.

TONIA. *(To Concepción, motioning toward the window:)* Look, they're trying to start something. Did you see that auto that went by? They're trying to stir up our people.

CONCEPCIÓN. Yes, yes, that's the truth. Tell Don Buena those people are trying to make trouble for us. *(Juan, hearing this, puts the table down and goes to the window.)* Quick! Go and tell him. *(Tonia goes out, rear, to the right.)* I think I'll go home.

MARIANA. *(Another woman of the people, entering rear, from the right.)* Juan, I have not been able to get Ernesto's shoes yet.

CONCEPCIÓN. *(Interrupting.)* Mariana, look how ugly things are getting out there. I think I'll go home.

MARIANA. Oh, Virgin of Perpetual Help! If Ernesto were only here! *(Juan, with a gesture of disillusion at what is taking place below and of disgust at the attitude of the women, returns to his table.)*

CONCEPCIÓN. *(To Juan:)* This is beginning to look bad. It looks as if there's going to be a riot. I think I'd better go home.

JUAN. There won't be anything of the kind! Those roughnecks are a bunch of cowards. Now let me alone. All of you get out of this room. *(He despairs at seeing Borracho.)*

BORRACHO. *(Entering rear from the left, in the passageway.)* Long live Don Buenaventura Padilla! *(Shouting.)* Tonia! Tonia! . . . Where are you, Tonia? Long live Don Buenaventura Padilla! *(He goes out, rear, to the right.)*

PEÑITA. *(Followed by the Second Man, enters rear from the right, running to the window.)* What's going on?

CONCEPCIÓN. They're stirring our people up from an automobile. I think I'll . . .

PEÑITA. *(Making sure at the window.)* But they're gone already. No need to be frightened by such a small thing. They're gone already . . .

TORTILLITA. *(Enters running from the right with the First Man.)* Here come our electors from Cibuco. They're in the backstreet.

FIRST MAN. Yes, yes, they're there. There're about four hundred of them.

JUAN. We'll have to father them in Manco Benito's shop. Tell Ventura. *(Through the rear, right, go out the First and Second Man, Tortillita, Peñita, and Concepción, saying:)*

FIRST MAN. Hail Mary, this is going to be good!

TORTILLITA. We'll win because we'll win!

SECOND MAN. Long live Don Buena!

ALL. Long may he live! *(Gabble of voices within upon their arrival, after which enter First and Third Man center from the right.)*

FIRST MAN. To Manco Benito's shop!

THIRD MAN. Let's go! *(Calling down the passageway to Tortillita, who has remained behind inside.)* Come on, Tortillita.

FIRST MAN. Come on! Long live Don Buena! *(He goes out running, right, followed by the Third Man.)*

TORTILLITA. *(Enters running center, right, and goes to the door right, but stops at Peñita's call.)*

PEÑITA. *(Enters center, right, calling:)* Tortillita, wait! They want you here. Let the others follow. *(Peñita goes out center, right, followed by Tortillita, who goes grumbling.)*

BORRACHO. *(Enters center, right, followed by Tonia, and yells out in the passageway:)* Long live Don Buenaventura Padilla! *(Coming into the room.)* Long live Don Buenaventura Padilla!

TONIA. Let's get out of here, Chencho, you're in a noisy mood . . .

BORRACHO. Leave me alone. Tonia, leave me alone, leave me alone . . . Long live Don Buenaventura Padilla! *(A bugle call sounds within. The drunk gives a military salute and goes back to his vivas, while Tonia little by little drags him to the door at the right.)*

JUAN. Get out, get out, I need this room. *(To Mariana who has seated herself on the bench:)* Please be so kind, Mariana. *(The drunk and Tonia go out right, struggling.)*

MARIANA. Jesus, Villegas, you sure are a pain today! *(She goes out center, right. Juan closes the center door so that no more pests shall enter and draws the table near the window, but the door opens slowly and a ridiculous man in dark glasses sticks his nose in, with a sign on his chest that says "TOURIST, HELP THE BLIND" and a sort of metal cup in his left hand to receive alms. He takes off his glasses and calls:)*

BLIND MAN. Psst, Villegas. *(Juan turns and gives him a terrible look, making a gesture for him to get out, so that the Blind Man withdraws rapidly, intimidated, closing the door behind him. Juan, who has turned his back, exclaims after the other has gone:)*

JUAN. Outside! I don't want anybody here now! *(As he is about to move the table again, he goes quite near the window and receives noisy applause and vivas! from the people below in the street, to whom he replies:)* Long live the Workers Party! Long live Buenaventura Padilla! *(The door at the back flies open, and there enter the Blind Man and the Bugler.)*

BUGLER. *(After blowing the bugle once is going to speak but has lost his voice. He makes an effort and says in a whisper:)* Hurray! . . . *(He climbs to the edge of the window.)*

BLIND MAN. If you go on shouting, you are going to lose your voice.

BUGLER. *(After a heroic effort makes himself understood.)* Hurray! for the defender of our daughters' virtues. *(Blows the bugle once. The vivas! from the street can be heard.)*

BLIND MAN. Hurray!

JUAN. Outside! Outside! Don Buenaventura Padilla is having his breakfast here. Let him rest for a minute; he has not closed his eyes for the last twenty-four hours. And you *(Referring to the Bugler.)*, leave the darn bugle alone; it's four in the morning. *(Puts them out and closes the door, reinforcing it with a chair. The bugle can be heard from the outside and is breaking his eardrums. As he approaches the window to get the table, he gets more applause from the street and yells out:)* Comrades, at last we are going to wipe out Don Ramón Torres and his gang. Hurray for Don Buenaventura Padilla, our Master! *(After Juan gets hold of the table, Carmela comes in through the door at the right, a beautiful, sweet youngster, who wants to be a practical woman. She brings in the breakfast service.)*

CARMELA. *(Trying to find a place where to put the breakfast.)* The place has not been fixed up yet, Juan?

JUAN. *(Hurries to help her.)* Carmelita! I'll fix everything right away. Here, give it to me, let me do it.

CARMELA. No, no. Put the typewriter away first. On the floor! If Father sees you! He loves that machine more than he does me! *(Juan picks up the typewriter and with great care sets it on a chair.)* What have you been doing all this time? I bet you were asleep, now, almost at dawn . . .

JUAN. *(Cleaning the table in a hurry and helping to set up the breakfast.)* Don't scold me, you know very well it took you a long time to go downstairs and ask Doña Zoila for this coffee. Everything is ready. This little draft . . . No! This is not the place for the table!

CARMELA. *(Teasing.)* Godfather Juan . . .

JUAN. For twenty years I have been your father's bodyguard. Am I or am I not? Come here, sit down. *(Absentmindedly he removes the chair he previously put against the door and makes her sit down.)* Nobody appointed me, nobody ever paid me a cent for it, and God forbid anybody from offering me money! But *(With pride.)* I am Don Buenaventura's bodyguard. Since the first pier strike twenty years ago!

CARMELA. Seventeen. *(Interrupting Juan before he can start to argue.)* It was when the police killed my mother.

JUAN. Jails, persecutions, clubbings . . . scars . . . *(Looks for an old scar on his head.)* With this one Tirado was promoted to a sergeant.

CARMELA. *(With friendly irony.)* And the one over . . . here? *(She runs her finger from one side to the other of his stomach.)*

JUAN. Well, that one was with a barbed wire, running away . . .

CARMELA. Godfather Juan, what will be your finish?

JUAN. Do you think that after seventeen years I am going to allow a man who has gone for twenty-four hours without sleep, making the last preparations for today's elections, come into an innocent gust of dawn that lovingly nears him, lovingly plays on his back . . . *(Pointing out the nearness of the table to the window.)* and . . . *(As if of a sudden the air had turned him to ashes.)* Paf!

CARMELA. You exaggerate. *(Going to serve the coffee.)*

JUAN. I exaggerate where the Master is concerned! *(Sweetening his expression.)* Carmela, my dear godchild, the university has not ruined you! Has it? *(Despicably.)* The university! Books! Books! Bah, paper! Here *(Touching his heart.)*, have they filled you with paper here?

CARMELA. *(Reproaches him, smiling, and pulls his nose.)* Oh, stop the foolishness! Fortunately, Father doesn't mind cold coffee . . .

JUAN. Anyway, it's good that you took a secretarial course at the university. The Master needs one. *(Confidentially and with dislike.)* Because the secretary he has . . . that Jaime Yepes . . . *(Sarcastically.)* his favorite pupil . . . *(Jaime enters from the right, a young man of uncultured manners who pretends to be refined, with affected gravity and superiority that marks with distaste all that surrounds him. Juan, fearful of having been overheard, displays a confused smile.)* Hello, Jaime! Did you give orders for the other car to be downstairs? *(He points to the right. Jaime nods.)*

CARMELA. I'll tell Father. *(She leaves by the door Jaime left open. Juan, seeing the Bugler and the Blind Man approaching, runs to close the door and reinforces it with the chair.)*

JAIME. Ah, coffee! *(He sits down to the table.)* Can it be the watery coffee made by the lady on the first floor?

JUAN. *(Nears him as if to squash him but goes to the window.)* Yes, yes, you're right. Your back a little more to this side. *(He opens the window wider.)* Comfortable, eh? Stay. *(Changes his tone.)* But don't touch a thing. Not even a cracker!

JAIME. Come now, man! I've been up all night the same as you, organizing our people for today's elections. Are you also going to turn traitor to the ideals of equality among men?

JUAN. Equality! Exactly! At your age the Master didn't have breakfast. It was when no shipper would give him work as they considered him dangerous. What does this new generation know of the Master's first political triumphs! At first he was alone . . . alone! Then I joined him. Later others followed. And then came the great test, the pier strike . . . Now there are even clubs . . . clubs of the Labor Party all over. Luxurious clubs like this one *(Gesture of incomprehension and then displeasance by Jaime.)* paid for punctually, no more than six months behind . . . Pictures . . . Typewriters . . . *(Jaime continues despective gestures.)* . . . Like this one.

JAIME. *(With sarcasm.)* Dust it off.

JUAN. *(Mechanically obeys with a handkerchief as he continues.)* And the election days like today. *(Puts the handkerchief away in a rage, realizing Jaime has been poking fun at him.)* The dawn would find us at the table of operations or in the jail, not stretched out in comfortable chairs. *(The chair he sits on breaks.)*

JAIME. Is someone calling? *(Carmelita can be heard calling Godfather Juan to open the door.)*

JUAN. *(Through the door.)* Carmelita? Yes, it's them. *(The Bugler can be heard. Juan calls to Jaime so loudly he jumps to his feet.)* Up, and put that table over there. *(While Jaime places the table on the right side of the room, Juan opens the door. Coming up the passageway surrounded by a group of comrades who push to get near him is Buenaventura Padilla, a man of fifty years of age, frank, sincere, authoritative, generous, plain, gruff, who likes to hear himself because he can't avoid thinking himself a great man. His spirit keeps him going even though he has labored all through the night. Followed by Carmela, he comes in fixing his shirt, saying to his companions something like: "Calm down, calm down, I'll fix everything," but his words can't be distinguished due to the noise made by the others. Juan, a little late and coolly helped by Jaime, tries to keep the group out of the room.)* No. No, you can't come in. No, no, you can't. *(The Bugler and Blind Man try to force an entrance.)* Out!

BUGLER AND BLIND MAN. *(Shout.)* We have to talk to Don Buena.

JUAN. Ventura, shall I let those two in?

BUENAVENTURA. *(Magnanimously.)* As you like. I am indifferent. *(Enter the Bugler, playing his instrument in triumph, and the Blind Man, followed by Peñita, Concepción, and Mariana, who slip in despite all of Juan's efforts. The two men go over to the bench to whisper.)*

JUAN. *(To one of those who tries to enter:)* You, you, I name you Guard. Don't allow anyone to enter without the Master's consent. *(The Guard, proud of his appointment, closes the door, remaining outside with the rest of the group, which still echoes, "Long live Buenaventura Padilla!")*

BUENAVENTURA. *(To Carmelita:)* Now! Why have you brought me to the library?

BUGLER. Library?

BUENAVENTURA. *(Pointing to the chair full of books.)* Library. A blind man can see that.

BLIND MAN. *(To Buenaventura's amazement.)* Yes, I see it.

BUENAVENTURA. I've made a blind man see! *(The Blind Man removes his glasses for a moment.)*

PEÑITA. *(To Buenaventura:)* You remember me, don't you? I am Peñita. *(He becomes annoyed upon being interrupted.)*

CARMELA. Father, what we want is for you to have your breakfast here, where you can be more relaxed. *(To the Bugler, who has resumed his playing:)* Please keep quiet now. *(To Buenaventura:)* Take your medicine as you may not have time later.

JUAN. Oh yes! Here it is! *(He takes the medicine from his pocket and places it on the tray.)*

BUENAVENTURA. *(Indignant, points to Juan.)* I bet this has been his idea. I'm in fine shape for banquets now. *(Shivering with distaste as he pronounces the word.)* Banquets! Is it really true, without exaggeration, that banquets are celebrated in the world? Remember, the day you see Buenaventura Padilla at a banquet, that day . . .

CARMELA. Father, this is your breakfast.

BUENAVENTURA. Breakfast, me? Alone? And all these people and the others *(Pointing to those who couldn't get in.)* and those downstairs and those who are coming along the road without sleep to vote for me. *(Pointing to some of those present.)* Don't you see them? They're about to drop in the arms of Orpheus.

CARMELA. *(Murmurs.)* With m, Father.

BUENAVENTURA. *(Correcting himself.)* Of Orpheum.* *(Over his protests Carmela takes him toward the table and begs him to be seated. She has almost succeeded when Buenaventura sees Peñita put the typewriter on the floor in order to sit on the chair.)* No! My typewriter! *(He picks it up tenderly.)* Carmelita, dear daughter, this is a struggle of ideals. It's the fight of the poor against the powerful. A fight! You all know what a fight is. In a fight neither side wants to lose. Result? Result: That both tries to win. And if we're fighting for the oppressed, am I going to stop for half an hour the launch of my ideals in the field of combat while I stuff myself? *(He places the typewriter on the table. Juan makes notes in a small notebook, without Buenaventura noticing.)* What are your pretensions? That they throw us on to the tragic beach where the sepulchers, in which cold remnants of the corpses of those who conform

*Buenaventura does not know the classical allusion is to Morpheus, the Greek god of sleep/dreams.

with living like slaves, rest? (*To Carmelita, who subtly and finally succeeds in making him sit.*) What fluency! Eh? How I can manage the language! Without universities! (*The handle of the cup is at the left-hand side, with which hand he raises it.*) Next time, remember I am not left-handed. Bring me a cup with the handle on the right side. (*Carmela in good humor turns the cup halfway.*) Ah! (*Coming out of his astound satisfaction, with anger again.*) But what time do I have for . . . (*The idea coming back to him.*) for banquets? . . . (*Gestures for the word.*) Banquets! . . . (*Coming back to reality. To Carmelita:*) What time do I have for breakfast when right now he has come to tell me . . . (*Points to Peñita, who tries to get close to him.*) No, no, it was not you . . . Now that someone has come to tell me our people from Hato Arriba cannot come to town because the others are waiting by the river to club them? How about the judges at the polls? And the bails for the incriminators? And you (*To Concepción who is trying hard to tell him something:*), say, what do you want? Don't speak to me if it isn't about ideals!

CONCEPCIÓN. I came to vote for you illegally, Don Buena . . . (*Gesture of approval from Don Buena, more noise in the street.*) I have been stopped because I am not of age, but Mother says that I have to vote for you . . . Because she says that for one that does not have the necessities, the best thing is to get a job with enough pay to supply a decent living. And the day we win . . . Mother, you know her, Concha . . . the leader of Garbanzo, our suburb . . . and my name is Concepción.

BUENAVENTURA. Ah, very good! Juan, look for the illegal card file in the living room.

JAIME. Bah! Principles! Ideals! (*Makes a gesture of dislike.*)

GUARD. (*Opens the door and shouts:*) Here is a reporter.

BUENAVENTURA. Don't let him in.

JUAN. I'll see him readily. *(To the Bugler, who had fallen asleep:)* You, come and bring the cards. *(Both come out rear right.)*

BUENAVENTURA. *(Getting up and nearing Jaime.)* This election is going to be honest. The only thing we will do is to put back the votes they steal from us. *(To the Blind Man:)* What do you want?

PEÑITA. *(Failing in his interruption.)* I am Peñita. You . . .

BLIND MAN. I . . . I am not registered . . . But I want to vote illegally for you . . . even if I have to give up my business for the day.

BUENAVENTURA. And what is your business?

BLIND MAN. My business is collecting alms. I make believe I am blind.

BUENAVENTURA. Without really being blind?

BLIND MAN. Well, you are not going to pretend that I poke out my eyes for a beastly alm! With what those tight bums give! The reason I am voting for you is to see to it that a bill is introduced placing a minimum for alms and tips!

BUGLER. *(Enters from the right with a big box on his head and tries to interrupt to explain, but he has lost his voice again and cannot make himself understood.)*

BUENAVENTURA. What is this man saying?

BLIND MAN. *(Taking charge, to his delight.)* He says that I am a man who makes an honest living begging.

BUGLER. *(Finally making himself heard.)* We brought him to vote illegally. But Villegas has given him the registration pertaining to a lawyer.

BLIND MAN. And he won't change it.

BUENAVENTURA. And why should he change it?

BLIND MAN. Look at me, Master, do you think that at this late date I can pass for a lawyer?

BUENAVENTURA. Perfectly. You will represent an honest lawyer.

JUAN. *(Enters alarmed from the door at the rear.)* Ventura! Ventura! We are in danger.

BUENAVENTURA. *(Serene amidst the general consternation.)* Bah, my twenty years of struggle have made me accustomed to having Demosthenes's sword over my head!

CARMELA. *(Whispering to him.)* Damocles, Father ...

BUENAVENTURA. Yours may be Damocles, Daughter, but mine is Demosthenes.

JUAN. Colmenero, the reporter from *The Voice* ...

BUENAVENTURA. *(Belittling.)* A yellow newspaperman who always publishes my manifestations full of geographic and prosaic mistakes.

CARMELA. Father, it's just that we make some changes when we type them ...

PEÑITA. *(Pulling Buenaventura's arm.)* I am ...

JUAN. Colmenero has come to ask your opinion regarding the last issue.

BUENAVENTURA. You very well know my opinion on the last issue. Did you tell him? *(Correcting himself.)* What is the last issue?

JUAN. That Don Ramón Torres, in person, has taken to the street. *(Those present break into exclamations: "Ah! Don Ramón! Now what!" There is a silence. Buenaventura takes a few pensive steps and lets himself fall into a chair.)*

CARMELA. *(With anguish.)* Don Ramón! No, no. Impossible!

JUAN. What's the matter, Carmela?

CARMELA. *(With a gesture which shows that nothing is wrong. Then almost to herself:)* It can't be. Anyone else, but not he. *(Jaime, who has gotten to his feet, studies her, intrigued. She sits down, lost in her thoughts.)*

BUENAVENTURA. *(To the Bugler:)* Let Colmenero pass. *(The Bugler jumps toward the back to carry out the order, but stops right away because Colmenero, a fresh, bold type of person who talks very fast, enters through the door at right.)*

COLMENERO. Don't be alarmed. My time is limited. *(As he passes, he takes a cracker from the table.)* They wouldn't let me in, so I went downstairs, went around, and came in the back door, I came up, and in I walked, and now that I am here, I want you to tell me quickly: What front are you going to put up to Don Ramón? *(He starts to eat the cracker.)*

CARMELA. *(Arising, can no longer hold back.)* Don Ramón is not taking part in this struggle!

BUENAVENTURA. Don Ramón! Always he against us! Always multiplied and subdivided against us. Be it one candidate or another who steals the elections from us, Don Ramón is always behind it, with his money, with his influence. Don Ramón, owner of banks, factories, shops, monopolies! The powerful man who seventeen years ago ordered the police to fire on the workers at his piers because we asked for more bread . . . and there fell beside me, shot through the stomach . . . a poor woman . . . that sainted innocent woman!

CARMELA. *(Begging him to stop.)* Father!

JUAN. *(Without being able to write in the notebook he had quickly taken out.)* Yes, Ventura, please don't remind me of the horrible killing of this one's mother.

BUENAVENTURA. *(Sweetly, upon seeing Carmela on the verge of tears.)* No, I harbor no remorse. I am not a man who likes to recall the unforgettable times, nor to float the horse of the battle of hate. *(Indignant.)* But as long as there are servants of the masses, hungry unfortunates, oppressed who cry for justice, I'll not go back. And the only road to be followed, are four: *(Counting on his fingers.)* Strikes in his factories, protests against his franchises, sabotage in his shops, fires on his farms. Ah, and the winning of this election! *(Quickly recounts on his fingers.)* Five! *(His audience noisily approves. Directing himself to Juan who is writing in the notebook.)* And you, what are you writing?

JAIME. *(Who has resumed his seat, speaks over his shoulder.)* Now he notes down your phrases so that he can repeat them when he speaks from the rostrum as being his own. *(Buenaventura swells with pride.)*

JUAN. So that they will not be lost . . .

COLMENERO. Then I can publish that . . .

BUENAVENTURA. *(With a smile that says, "And I still haven't let myself go!")* Submerged in the tempest-tossed sea of this electionary volcano . . . eh, Juan? *(Starts to walk, gloating at his words while Juan makes notes.)* We search the horizon for the lifeboat . . . eh? . . . and under its roof . . . *(To Peñita, who doesn't know what more to do to attract his attention.)* Yes, you are Peñita . . . *(Continuing magnificently, as if nothing has interrupted him.)* and under its roof we open the doors of refuge . . . like shipwrecked people who still have no thoughts of capsizing . . . How I manage the language!

COLMENERO. Which means . . .

BUENAVENTURA. What do you mean "Which means"?

COLMENERO. Where is the boat?

BUENAVENTURA. What boat?

CARMELA. *(To Colmenero:)* Just write that Father will maintain an attitude of expectancy . . .

BUENAVENTURA. You always get your own way! *(In bad humor.)* Alright. *(Once again magnificent.)* Put down that we will maintain ourselves in an expectorant attitude.

COLMENERO. Wait? Is that all? And for that you have made me lose so much time here? Wait?

BUENAVENTURA. When something occurs to me, I never fail.

COLMENERO. Wait! With the Editor insisting on news for an extra! I'll come back in a little while . . . by this same entrance. *(Indicates the door at the right, by which he leaves.)*

BUENAVENTURA. Yes, yes, that way. *(As soon as Colmenero has gone, he says to Peñita, who is trying to make himself seen:)* You, Peñita, go and guard the downstairs door and don't let him up. *(He sits down to the table. Peñita, the Blind Man, the Bugler, Mariana, and Concepción gather tightly around him, all trying to talk at the same time.)*

PEÑITA. First I want to tell you my brother will die . . . *(Down in the street something has happened, judging from the sudden profound silence, which is followed immediately by outcries. This is due to the fact that a very important person has just arrived, gotten out of his automobile, and is at the moment coming up the stairs. Carmela, who has looked out the window, is pale and can hardly control her emotions.)* Yes, my brother will die if he does not vote against these lowly thieves . . .

MARIANA. I also want to tell you that my husband Ernesto . . .

PEÑITA. My brother, you know, is very vain . . .

MARIANA. My husband Ernesto, the poor thing, has of late been having fevers.

CONCEPCIÓN. My registration card, Mother is waiting for me . . .

GUARD. *(From the door at the rear which he opens a little.)* Here is a gentleman who wants to see you, Master.

JAIME. *(Who had been looking for Concepción's card.)* A gentleman! That dope still believes in gentlemen! Let him wait!

DON RAMÓN. *(Jaime's order has been useless. Pushing the Guard to one side, Don Ramón Torres enters, a capitalist of about fifty, used to giving orders, well dressed, underlining his importance with a cane and a chronic cough. Carmela muffles a scream. Buenaventura and those around him do not realize the newcomer's presence until he is in middle of the room and announces himself by tapping on the floor with his cane and coughing. Concepción, Mariana, the Bugler, the Blind Man, and Peñita step to the back with great respect. Jaime, leaving the card file, stands indignant. Juan, near to Carmela, does not understand what has happened. Buenaventura rises. The Guard, curious, leaves the door open a little and, hearing the first words, decides to remain between the two door halves. Don Ramón, who is furious, tries to control himself.)* Buenaventura Padilla? You, no? *(Buenaventura nods.)* I am Ramón Torres, at your service.

BUENAVENTURA. *(Jumps as if he had been given an electric shock.)* The one from the banks? The one from the piers? Don Ramón? *(He goes near to him and touches him.)* Will you allow me to touch you first? I had almost thought it impossible. *(To the others:)* He is a man! A skin and bone man!

DON RAMÓN. *(Referring to those around.)* Can we speak quietly . . . here?

BUENAVENTURA. *(With a wave, signals to his people to the left of the room, from where some look and others talk among themselves. Peñita makes fun of Don Ramón, imitating his gestures and cough and making the others laugh, which causes Don Ramón to become nervous at times. Carmela and Jaime remain together by the window. Buenaventura offers his chair to Don Ramón, placing it at the extreme left of the table. He takes another chair for himself and is about to place it beside the other when he thinks better of it and places it at the extreme right.)* I have been so anxious to meet you personally . . . for some seventeen years!

DON RAMÓN. *(Controlling his fury.)* You have called more than fifty strikes in my factories. And the damage you have caused by sabotage and malicious fires goes into many millions of dollars.

BUENAVENTURA. Is that all? *(Laugh caused by Peñita.)*

DON RAMÓN. Do you realize that all I would have had to do is step aside and any one of my foremen would have done away with you?

BUENAVENTURA. *(Distracted.)* Yes? *(On the alert, realizing the threat.)* Eh?

DON RAMÓN. Right now you force me for the first time in my life to come down personally to the mudhole of politics . . .

BUENAVENTURA. Oh, don't come down! Leave this mudhole for me alone . . . *(Lots of laughter caused by Peñita. Carmela calls his attention and tells him not to continue.)*

DON RAMÓN. You have taken to the use of illegal voting just like us. And that is not fair! The minority should know how to be the minority . . . *(Carmela takes a few steps forward to take part in the conversation but restrains herself, full of anguish.)*

BUENAVENTURA. This time remember that this prediction is going to be carried out right to the number. Our majority is going to be three out of every four . . . *(At the door the Guard has a discussion with two who are trying to force an entrance.)*

GUARD. No, no.

JUAN. *(Coming to the rescue.)* Out, pests! Out!

DON RAMÓN. Fortunately, my friends have advised me while there is still time. I have distributed my personal agents all over. Here, in your district, the most important for us, your comrades of Hato Arriba have already been disbanded. Half of your poll attendants have sold you out. Right now my people were going to disband the voters you have concentrated at Manco Benito's shop.

BUENAVENTURA. Even with all that . . . we will deliver the blow of your downfall.

DON RAMÓN. All the worse for you.

BUENAVENTURA. Worse?

DON RAMÓN. That's what I came to tell you. Between life and death there is only one step, a simple, insensible step . . . *(Juan keeps Carmela back.)* Through me yesterday we drafted six gunmen.

BUENAVENTURA. *(Distracted.)* Only six? *(Terrified.)* Eh! Six! Would you dare . . . ?

DON RAMÓN. Gunmen have a very odd way of expressing their gratitude . . .

BUENAVENTURA. *(Drying his forehead.)* Yes? *(The Blind Man is going to beg alms of Don Ramón. Buenaventura makes a gesture as if to strike him, and the Blind Man erroneously believes himself in danger and retires so quickly that it causes Don Ramón's surprise.)*

DON RAMÓN. I am a man who knows how to win, and I know how to lose, and I know how to bargain . . . And I know how to allow my friends to win their tokens of gratitude. Do I make myself clear?

BUENAVENTURA. *(Hoarsely.)* You still have a little . . . *(Correcting himself.)* Yes, yes, absolutely clear . . . You make yourself disphanously clear.

DON RAMÓN. I have come here to serenely inform you before arriving at a conclusion. *(Pushes aside what is on the table and rests his elbows on same.)* I want to know what you plan to do if you win this election.

BUENAVENTURA. *(Takes inventory of his courage, stands, coughs loudly, walks to and fro, swallows.)* Well . . . expect . . .

PEÑITA. *(Interrupting.)* I beg your pardon, Don Buena, but I must go. What's been decided about the suit?

BUENAVENTURA. Suit?

PEÑITA. For my brother . . . who is very vain . . . he is not going looking like a tramp to vote for the defender of the honesty of the government.

JUAN. *(Interrupting.)* All there was to give was used up since midnight . . . you know that, Peñita . . .

BUENAVENTURA. *(To Peñita:)* Here, here. Let him be satisfied with half . . . *(He removes his jacket.)* And this . . . the first brand-new tie I ever wore in my life.

JUAN. *(Taking the jacket and tie from Peñita.)* Give me that. *(To Buenaventura:)* Let him wait. Finish there and later we'll talk of this. *(Makes Peñita retire.)*

BUENAVENTURA. *(To Don Ramón, trying to get him on the new subject:)* A suit . . . He wants a suit . . . Jacket, pants . . . A suit . . .

DON RAMÓN. *(Getting to the point.)* You still haven't answered my question.

BUENAVENTURA. *(Gradually becoming resolute.)* Ah, yes, your question! Oh, yes . . . as I was saying . . . I am a man who does nothing hidden. You want to know what we are going to do when we win. I am going to tell you. Be prepared to hear the worse. You have some land near here which is a center for malaria. Do you have it or don't you? You have it, don't you? Swampy land? Well, then. *(Dropping his gestures.)* I plan . . . to dry them up. *(Aggressive again.)* On your farms there is too much anemia. Your workers are pale, sick. Yes, no? Yes! Well, I plan . . . to cure them. They'll be able to work more. And all those with TB you have in your factories, whom you don't dare to fire because of your fear or their despair, all those . . . will go to a sanatorium I plan to build. There will be big hospitals and many industrial schools and vocational schools where the government will train the personnel you need in your factories.

DON RAMÓN. *(Arising.)* Fine! And the strikes?

BUENAVENTURA. I am also going to pass legislation to end strikes, and there will not be the slightest sign of sabotage left. *(The listeners show signs of surprise. Juan asks Carmela with gestures if Buenaventura has gone crazy, and Jaime shakes himself top to bottom, displaying his distaste.)*

DON RAMÓN. Tell me, how do you plan to do all these things: hospitals, schools, sewerage, sanatoriums?

BUENAVENTURA. *(Serenely, after making a supreme call on his courage.)* Oh! . . . with taxes . . .

DON RAMÓN. With taxes?

BUENAVENTURA. With the taxes I am going to make you pay. *(The Bugler makes a noise with his instrument.)*

DON RAMÓN. *(Furious but keeping himself under control.)* And the strikes? . . . How are you going to end the strikes?

BUENAVENTURA. I am going to pass legislation prohibiting the payment of starvation wages. *(Don Ramón hits the table so hard with his cane that the cup jumps.)* My coffee! *(Looking at the typewriter.)* My typewriter! Anything, but don't touch that typewriter!

DON RAMÓN. I am going to give you an alternative and you are going to answer yes or no . . .

BUENAVENTURA. No.

DON RAMÓN. You haven't heard it yet.

BUENAVENTURA. No! No! No to anything! Do what you like. The next step is in your hands.

CARMELA. Don Ramón . . . please, that's enough . . .

DON RAMÓN. *(Looks at her solemnly for a minute. There are mixed emotions and tears in her eyes. He is going to answer. No. He turns to Buenaventura. With threatening courtesy:)* Until later. *(He leaves by the rear door which is opened by the Guard who remains between the two halves, while a ridiculous tune is played on the bugle. Those present acclaim Buenaventura: "Well done! That's the way to do it! Long live the Master!" The Guard remains outside as he closes the door.)*

BUENAVENTURA. How stupid talented men can be. Kill me! Bah! As if I would fear a death previously announced in advance! Cowardness has a . . . has a antithesis. *(Mispronounced: "anti-thesis.")* Cowardness, don't forget, has a *(Accentuating the word.)* antithesis: that of not being cowardly. They can trample me, but I'll not run away. *(Juan looks for his notebook.)* Make notes, Juan . . . make notes . . . They kill me and what happens? There is Jaime. *(Juan puts his notebook away with indignation.)* And there is Juan, my most faithful friend . . . *(Juan, enchanted, again brings out his notebook.)* My blood, hear me, my blood . . .

CONCEPCIÓN. My card . . . I want to go home . . .

MARIANA. *(Interrupting.)* As I was telling you about Ernesto . . . with that fever he can't go to vote barefooted. If there was a pair of shoes . . .

BUENAVENTURA. Will these fit him? *(He sits on the chair to remove the ones he has on.)*

JUAN. *(Stopping him.)* Ventura, please! And put on your coat, here. In your shirtsleeves! A party leader! *(The noise from the street increases.)*

PEÑITA. My brother needs a suit . . .

BUENAVENTURA. *(To Juan, referring to the coat:)* Give it to him. *(He gets up and takes it from Juan who hesitates and gives it to Peñita.)* Here. It is made of the best English vineyard wool.

PEÑITA. And the pants?

BUENAVENTURA. *(Looks at his own. It seems like he is going to take them off right on the spot. He looks at the pants on Juan, who looks full of terror as Buenaventura nears him to touch them.)* Pants?

JUAN. *(With a scream, protecting his.)* No! *(The Guard opens the door at the rear and pushes in four or five persons accompanied by a laborer who has his head tied with a bloody bandage. Those in the room gather at the door.)*

BUENAVENTURA. I suspect. In Manco Benito's workshop, no? Defending our voters from the Cibuco? *(The Wounded Man nods his head.)* Well, let's go there right now. *(The Bugler, who is at the window, plays his instrument and vivas are heard.)*

BLIND MAN. *(Calling from the window:)* Get ready to follow the Master. *(Shots are heard from the street. The Blind Man, the Bugler, and those with them near the window protect themselves, some dropping to the floor. Someone shouts, "We've been fired upon!" Concepción and Mariana run out the right rear, screaming, and return after it is all over. From the rear right and left enter some very solicitous comrades. During the firing Juan has held Buenaventura back from going to the window.)*

BUENAVENTURA. Criminals! Assassins! Abels! Abels! Abels who want to again kill Cain!

BUGLER. *(Arising and pointing to the roof.)* There it is . . . That's where it went in.

BLIND MAN. *(Arising.)* The shooting was done from an automobile that went by like mad. I saw the whole thing.

BUENAVENTURA. *(Goes to the window and calls:)* Anyone wounded down there? *(Vivas are heard.)* No one? *(From below they answer no one and the vivas are repeated.)*

BUENAVENTURA. *(To the Bugler:)* You! You should be wounded. Check yourself well.

BUGLER. *(Scared to death, starts to cry.)* Wounded!

BLIND MAN. *(Checking him over.)* No, he's whole.

BUGLER. Yes, yes. Whole! *(He plays the bugle.)* I'll inform the police. *(He runs to the rear door.)*

BUENAVENTURA. No. *(The Bugler stops.)* Do you want us arrested? *(To Jaime:)* You, get this girl's card. *(To Carmela, placing his hand under her chin affectionately:)* You won't go out of here, now, will you?

CARMELA. *(Hugging him.)* Father!

BUENAVENTURA. *(Giving her courage.)* What, afraid? The university has softened you? I don't know you. All your life you have been used to this. *(Carmela steps back, shakes her head while she dries her tears. To Juan:)* I will return soon.

JUAN. What do you mean, you'll return soon? Aren't I going? Me?

BUENAVENTURA. You say it as if you were my bodyguard. Come now, man! You know I haven't had one all my life; I should have one now that I'm getting old! You are needed here. *(To the others:)* Let's go, let's go. Viva the death of the big cacique! *(He leaves by the left door with vivas and bugle calls, followed by all, except Jaime, Concepción, Mariana, Juan, who is dumbfounded, and Carmela, who runs to the window to say goodbye. The door remains open and you can tell that the house is empty with exception of those in the room.)*

JAIME. *(Making fun.)* Seventeen years of service! Here, look for this girl's card, as I'm no good when it comes to hacking scruples. *(Lights a cigarette.)*

JUAN. Nor for anything. *(Looks among the cards.)* The redemption of the laborer should be the work of the laborer himself. Who is going to do it for us if we don't put in our own illegal voters? *(Takes out a card. Vivas are heard from the street and bugle calls go off into the distance.)*

CARMELA. There they go! *(Carmela starts to wave her handkerchief but realizes it is useless.)* They won't look back! Godfather Juan, just like that, with that same faith . . . to fight an injustice . . . Is that the way they marched that other day . . . seventeen years ago?

JUAN. *(Without answering, nears the window and calls:)* Long live the Mas— *(He does not finish the word because the street is silent and deserted.)* They have all gone with him! All of them, all of them except me. *(He throws the card to Jaime and runs out the rear, calling like a lunatic, as if those already gone could hear him.)* Wait for me! Wait for me!

JAIME. *(To Concepción, pointing to the card which is on the floor:)* Pick it up. *(She obeys.)*

CARMELA. *(Nears the table. Removes the medicine box from the tray and places it on the table. She gives the crackers to Concepción.)* Here, Concepción; give some to Mariana.

CONCEPCIÓN. Thank you, Carmelita.

CARMELA. *(To Jaime, picking up the tray to take the rest of the breakfast away:)* You couldn't eat it as it's ice cold.

JAIME. *(Calling her as she is about to leave.)* Carmela! *(She stops.)* Come back as soon as you take that. *(Carmela is surprised.)* I must talk to you. *(She shakes her head slowly and leaves by the right door. To Concepción, trying to get rid of her quickly:)* You know what you have to do, don't you? Do you know the signal so that our people at the polls will make no accusation? *(Concepción shakes her head.)* Well then, so long . . . *(To Mariana:)* So long . . . *(He turns his back. Concepción and*

Mariana leave by the left door, saying humbly: "Thank you, goodbye." When Jaime turns around, he finds George, who has entered by the left.) What do you want here?

GEORGE. *(A young man, agreeable, of executive type and distinguished carriage which is evident even though he is carelessly dressed: he does not have on a coat, hat, or tie.)* Where is Carmelita?

JAIME. What do you want for her?

GEORGE. *(Emphatically.)* Where is Carmelita?

JAIME. Who are you?

GEORGE. *(With more force.)* Where is Carmelita?

CARMELA. *(Entering from the right.)* George! You, here!

GEORGE. Carmelita! *(Goes to meet her.)* I have just arrived from the university . . . because of your letter. *(Noting her cold attitude.)* But what is the matter? *(Jealous of Jaime.)* Ah! This! *(With disgust.)* No, impossible. *(To Jaime:)* Will you please leave me alone for a minute . . . *(Calmly.)* with my sweetheart?

JAIME. *(Questions Carmelita with his eyes; she lowers hers.)* If it's that way . . .

CARMELA. *(Upset.)* No, no, it isn't that way!

GEORGE. *(Persuasively to Jaime:)* Please leave us alone for a minute.

JAIME. *(Thinks for a minute, raises his shoulders, and goes slowly to the rear door. To Carmela:)* I'll be outside.

GEORGE. Last night . . . that is . . . this very night, because it isn't dawn . . . I received your letter. *(He takes it from his pocket.)* Full of love. I couldn't sleep because of your word of possible disorder due to the elections. And sure enough upon my arrival I have been told there have been shots fired. *(Reacting to the block of ice which he has in front of him.)* One has to have a dog's luck . . . One gets out of bed, takes an automobile at midnight, eats up the road, violates traffic laws, climbs the steps three at a time to see if anything has happened to one's sweetheart, and finds her . . . finds her . . . *(He can't find words to express the transformation.)*

CARMELA. I appreciate your interest, but . . .

GEORGE. *(Waiting.)* But . . .

CARMELA. A wall has come up between us.

GEORGE. *(Following her.)* You're delirious.

CARMELA. No, it's just that at last I've awakened. One always awakens from dreams. You will continue at the university, George, but now I find myself out in the world, where dreams are forbidden.

GEORGE. I don't understand one word. *(From the letter.)* Just a few hours ago . . .

CARMELA. *(Leans against the table.)* At the university, in the commercial school of the university, we were two free souls, plain and happy . . . Me in my secretarial course, so that later I could help Father . . . You in your business administration course, big business, so that you may later take charge of your fortune . . . Yes, we could dream then . . . We could . . . love each other . . . We were, or thought we were, what life has said we are not: equals. *(Her voice breaks.)* A great wall stands between us, a wall of gold, George, which will always separate us. *(She turns her back to him, drops in a chair, and, placing her arms on the back, lets her head rest on them.)*

GEORGE. *(Again brings forth the letter and reads.)* "George, my George . . ." A few hours ago you said that. And here: "George, it is impossible to be happier than I am when I think that you love me." *(He turns the page and looks for the signature.)* "Your Carmelita."

CARMELA. *(Crying.)* Go, go.

GEORGE. *(Confused.)* How stupid I am! No, no, don't cry. It's just that I really don't know, I don't understand . . . Don't cry . . . Bah, don't pay any attention to me! I'm going. As you wish . . . *(He takes a few steps slowly toward the door and turns with a little hope.)* Without a word of explanation? *(As he receives no reply, he takes a few more steps, beaten, but suddenly regains control of himself.)* No, you love me. Here *(In the letter.)* you say you love me. You said it, didn't you? Isn't it true that you love me? Answer.

CARMELA. *(Arising, says definitely:)* Goodbye, George.

GEORGE. *(He crumples the letter in his fist and is about to throw it away, changes his mind, and shoves it into his pocket. Deeply hurt but still not wanting to leave.)* Listen to this oath I'm going to take . . . *(Jaime enters.)* No, nothing. *(He barely nods his head and leaves by the left. Carmela stands still for a moment, takes a few rapid steps toward the door to call him back, runs to the window, hesitates, sits down on the bench, and sobs.)*

JAIME. I believe he said . . . sweetheart?

CARMELA. *(After a brief pause, notes the daylight coming in the window.)* It won't be long before the sun comes out.

JAIME. *(Coming near her.)* He said . . . sweetheart?

CARMELA. *(Almost talking to herself, looking out of the window.)* A dream . . . a dream that disappeared with the dawn . . .

JAIME. *(Stepping back.)* Incomplete sale then . . . The smell of money is injuring my nostril . . .

CARMELA. *(Not paying much attention to him.)* It was a beautiful dream . . . It was a happy world in which blame fell on no one soul . . . There was no misery, no riches . . . Because what difference did it make, one thing or another?

JAIME. *(Standing near her.)* Carmela, have you forgotten what you are, what you think, what you feel?

CARMELA. What are you saying?

JAIME. Have you forgotten who your father is? The day that you give your heart, or that you are disloyal to yourself, or you choose a man of your class . . . of my class . . . a man like me . . .

CARMELA. *(Turning toward him.)* Like you?

JAIME. Why not? Don't we stand for equal rights? You might as well know it: I love you, Carmela.

CARMELA. *(Rising.)* You?

JAIME. Are you surprised? *(Walking behind her.)* Are you surprised to be loved by one who has not traded with the sweat of the laborers, who has not enjoyed the hunger of the others? Or it is that Buenaventura Padilla's daughter should prefer one who has his hands stained with fugitive blood?

CARMELA. *(Stopping.)* Quiet . . .

JAIME. We are both fortunately on this side of the golden wall.

CARMELA. *(Turning around, surprised.)* Ah! You were listening?

JAIME. But am I or am I not right?

CARMELA. *(Not daring to face him.)* You are right.

JAIME. Then you love me? Do you love me?

CARMELA. Keep quiet. My head is going around. Right now I don't know what I want. *(Hugging Buenaventura who enters from the left very fatigued, followed by Juan who has removed his coat and uselessly has tried to get Buenaventura to put it on.)* Father . . . Father . . .

BUENAVENTURA. Keep your spirit up, Daughter! Nothing has happened! *(To Juan through the bandage:)* I'm telling you that you put your head in wrong. That was coming for me and I could have stopped it. *(To Jaime:)* Take a telegram for the principal papers. *(To Juan, while Jaime looks for a notebook and pencil:)* I don't see the one with the glasses either.

JUAN. The Blind Man? The police got him as well as the Bugler. *(He throws the coat on the chair filled with rage because Buenaventura always gets away from him.)*

BUENAVENTURA. *(To Jaime:)* Ready? *(Dictating.)* By the present telegram written ad hoc . . . no, . . . By the present telegram signed by the signer . . . *(Explaining.)* or in other words myself, I ratify before the people, expecting their favorable verdict, my protest, for the terrible transgression . . . *(Mentally tries to find another adjective.)*

JUAN. Frightening . . .

BUENAVENTURA. More than frightening. *(Continues to look for the word.)* For the nonspeakable transgression!

CARMELA. *(Correcting.)* Unspeakable, Father?

BUENAVENTURA. No? Don't you like it? *(Dictates, annoyed.)* For the frightening trans— *(Again satisfied, slaps his forehead.)* horrific and unpolluted, which cannot remain harmless, of which the sergeant has made victims . . . *(To Juan:)* You have it on your head . . .

JUAN. *(Remembering and touching his scar.)* Sergeant Tirado.

BUENAVENTURA. . . . Sergeant Tirado and his police and friends, a group of pacific citizens who were at Benito Mejías's workshop, known as the "Lame" . . .

CARMELA. *(Correcting.)* Armless Mejías, Father.

BUENAVENTURA. It's that now they have given him a hailshot in a leg.

CARMELA. Then there were shots?

BUENAVENTURA. *(Correcting.)* Shot was fired.

CARMELA. Were.

BUENAVENTURA. How can you tell me? I was there and saw the whole thing with my own eyes. Shot was fired . . . plurals. I've got the exact speech down pat. *(Continues dictating.)* The complete group would have been mowed down and disbanded—and it was, after all—if it had not been for the help rendered by a mess of humanity which arrived from the Labor Party Club. Among the wounded . . . *(To Juan:)* The Bugler got a swollen face, no? *(Juan nods and Buenaventura continues.)* Figures a player of the art of music, who a policeman kicked . . . *(Correcting himself.)* who a pathogenic policeman gave a swollen carotid artery to . . . Also figures . . . *(To Juan who nods:)* The Blind Man came out nude, no? *(Continues dictating.)* Also figures a poor invalid of the solar light of the sun planet, who another agent assailed by authority, tore his clothes into pigments . . .

JUAN. *(In ecstasy, making notes.)* What a colossal way of saying that they got clubbings of all colors!

BUENAVENTURA. *(Dictating.)* The Blind Man was merely an ocular witness of the goings-on.

JUAN. Witness? Listen, Ventura, it was worthwhile to see the way he threw stones, the devil.

BUENAVENTURA. And now to close with a celebrated phrase so that they will see that here rests a brain . . . *(Dictating.)* In view of these transgressions which are being done to us in order to steal the elections from us, from the impermeable summit of ideals I ask for: "Freedom, freedom," as Cicero said upon ascending to the guillotine. Period. *(Colmenero enters right.)* What? By the back door again? *(Referring to the telegram.)* Copy to him. *(Juan has picked up the coat in order to try again to put it on Buenaventura.)*

COLMENERO. Copy? Of your will? *(Gives a quick glance out the window.)*

BUENAVENTURA. Copy of my will? *(Realizing.)* Eh?

COLMENERO. Yes, I want to know what the dispositions in your will are, but quickly, before it is too late . . . because there comes a gang to take this exclusive information away from me. *(Juan, confused, puts on his coat.)*

BUENAVENTURA. Gang of newspapermen?

COLMENERO. No, the gang that is coming to kill you.

PEÑITA. *(Enters running left, returning Buenaventura's coat and tie.)* I'm returning what's yours. No judge is going to grab me for wearing the coat belonging to a corpse . . . There they come . . . *(Goes out right like a flash. Carmela, nervous, goes to the window.)*

JUAN. *(Pushing Buenaventura toward the door, right.)* Let's go to the Rio Blanco Club . . . Quick . . . I alone can't protect you.

BUENAVENTURA. *(Wanting to appear serene.)* By the way you speak you sound as if you were my bodyguard . . .

JUAN. Let's not lose a minute! What do you want? Them to make mincemeat of you?

BUENAVENTURA. *(Without realizing, nods, but upon realizing, yells:)* No! *(Goes to Carmela, grabs her hand.)* Come, Carmela.

JUAN. So that she'll also stop a bullet if they fire at you along the street? Let her hide downstairs in Doña Zoila's house . . . Let's go to the Rio Blanco. To Rio Blanco!

BUENAVENTURA. *(Directing his steps to the door.)* They can push me around but I'll not run. *(Juan, Jaime, and Buenaventura leave right, but right away Buenaventura reenters, followed by Juan trying to make him leave again.)*

JUAN. Ventura, I admire your courage, but you must not remain here.

BUENAVENTURA. No, I just came back to take him too . . . (*To Colmenero:*) You . . . You're not staying behind in order to tell them where they must go to assassinate me.

COLMENERO. Don't be cruel! Don't you understand that this is the best exclusive news of the year?

JUAN. (*Grabbing Colmenero.*) Get going. (*Leaves right, forcing Colmenero.*)

BUENAVENTURA. Go downstairs, Carmela. Take good care . . .

JUAN. (*From inside.*) Ventura, it will be too late!

BUENAVENTURA. (*Gives a quick kiss to Carmela.*) Ah, nothing frightens you! You're just like your father. (*Starts to run to the door.*) God bless you, Daughter! (*Goes out right.*)

CARMELA. God spare you, Father! (*Goes to the window, makes a gesture of surprise. Starts to the door at rear by which enters George excited.*)

GEORGE. (*At the door.*) Did they go? Where are they?

CARMELA. That's what you'd like to know.

GEORGE. Tell me, tell me quickly, where are they?

CARMELA. So you may have the glory of assassinating them?

GEORGE. Are you crazy, Carmela? To save them. Tell me at least one place where they are not in order to save them. They are not at Sabana Seca? Yes? No? (*Gang enters left with clubs, knives, and firearms, accompanied by Sergeant Tirado.*)

GANG LEADER. (*Surprised.*) Don Georgito! Here! (*Believing he under stands.*) Ah! What a man! Wanted to beat us to it, eh? (*Proud.*) Alone, like a man! I'll tell this to your father. Where did they go?

GEORGE. (*Questioning Carmela with his eyes.*) To . . . Sabana . . . to Sabana Seca . . . (*One of the gang grabs the typewriter to take it with him.*)

CARMELA. *(Serene.)* I beg you to leave that machine in its place.

TIRADO. And this woman who is out of order? Can't you see that the police is here to keep order? You're under arrest. *(Takes a step to grab her.)*

GEORGE. *(Interposing himself, gives Tirado a hard push.)* Coward! *(The Gang Leader holds the Sergeant back, while George changes his tactics in order to save the situation.)* No, we don't lose time with women. To the men! To Sabana Seca!

TIRADO. *(To the Gang Leader:)* But who is he?

GANG LEADER. Him? He is Don Georgito . . . Don Ramón's son. *(Some of the gang repeat, surprised: "Don Ramón's son!")*

TIRADO. *(Confused.)* Don Ramón's son!

GEORGE. To Sabana Seca!

GANG LEADER. Let's go, let's go to give them a good beating in Sabana Seca.

GEORGE. To Sabana Seca! *(Leads the group, but remains in the hall, thus making the rest leave. The gang and Tirado leave left. Some yell: "To Sabana Seca!" Others upon passing look and stare at "Don Ramón's son." Carmela, thinking they have all gone, slowly nears the window.)*

CARMELA. Don Ramón's son! Buenaventura's daughter. *(Now the sun falls upon her as it comes in the window.)* A new sun arises!

GEORGE. *(Jumping forward to take her in his arms.)* Carmela! Carmelita! *(With her leaning against his chest.)* A new sun! A new sun shines upon the world!

CURTAIN

Left to right: Juan (Walter Busó), Concepción (Jennie Sosa), and Buenaventura Padilla (Benjamín Morales). From the 1966 production of *Mi señoría* presented by the Institute of Puerto Rican Culture (Instituto de Cultura Puertorriqueña) at the Tapia Theater in San Juan, Puerto Rico. Photograph courtesy of the Institute of Puerto Rican Culture—General Archives of Puerto Rico.

Second Act

The dazzling small living room—at its best it is even a little overdone—of the suite occupied by Buenaventura Padilla in a luxurious hotel. Telegrams thrown all over. Flowers. On the telephone table, a shorthand notebook, a pencil. At rear, a large entrance. A rug-covered staircase, a small hall which leads, to the right, to Carmela's room, at left, a door which leads to the elevator hall. Left lateral door which leads to Buenaventura's room. JUAN, reclining in a chair, and JAIME, standing, impatient, are in full dress ready to attend a banquet being given in honor of the Honorable Buenaventura Padilla, president of the Chamber of Deputies, at the same hotel, but as they couldn't stand the coats, they have taken them off and have placed them on chairs.

JUAN. The furniture in this hotel sure is something, eh? Smooth! Comfortable! Now I can understand why in each house no more than twelve persons live, while in a hotel of luxury like this, two or three thousand live.

JAIME. *(Very much annoyed.)* Bah! Effeminacy of the capitalist!

JUAN. What do they know of these things! You have to have tamed the benches of a dozen jails, like I have. And then . . . when one can name and discharge judges as one pleases, one comes and sits . . . *(Gives a yell of ecstasy.)* Ah! Tomorrow remind me. Now that we are in power, I am going to have a law put through to have the cells of all the jails furnished like this charming little room.

JAIME. You spoke more sensibly when our party was in the minority. Since we won, all you do is defend laws such as that one. What you want to do is join the criminals.

JUAN. *(Arising.)* No, no, just a moment. All the projects in which I have been interested have been presented and defended by the very president of the Chamber of Deputies. Listen good: The president of the Chamber of Deputies. Or is it that you are also going to speak badly of the president of the Chamber of Deputies? *(Answering a gesture from Jaime.)* Say it, go ahead and say it. Say that you believe His Honor, the president, to also be an idiot. Everyone worth anything in the country has come here tonight to his native town to a banquet in his honor, but you think that His Honor, the president, is an imbecile. An imbecile! The man to whom . . . There you have it . . . *(Pointing to the innumerable telegrams thrown in piles in different places.)* Telegrams sent from all places for His Excellency, the president. And what a reception his town has given him! *(Answering a gesture from Jaime.)* Don't swallow it. Talk.

JAIME. *(Annoyed.)* Mr. President! His Excellency, Mr. President! Bah! I am a man of ideals. I'm no good for these capitulations. Look at yourself, look at yourself . . .

JUAN. *(Looking at himself.)* Eh!

JAIME. A regular capitalist . . . The only thing you have to learn is to keep your coat on.

JUAN. Well . . . you too for that matter . . . *(He takes Jaime's coat and holds it as if the other were going to put it on, but Jaime pulls it out of his hand and throws it on a chair.)*

JAIME. *(Answering the telephone without paying attention to what is being said.)* No, the president of the Chamber of Deputies is not here. No one is here. I'm not here either. Don't bother us.

JUAN. *(Putting on his coat.)* Who was it?

JAIME. *(Annoyed.)* God only knows! Some other capitalist to pay homage!

JUAN. *(Taking a flower from a vase.)* Ah! Divine! These roses were not here a minute ago . . . *(Puts a flower in his buttonhole.)* Are these the ones Carmela was going to carry?

JAIME. *(Sitting.)* Yes. *(Upon noting the flower in Juan's buttonhole, makes a gesture of disgust.)* Even Carmela is becoming capitalistic.

JUAN. Leave my godchild out of this.

JAIME. You wouldn't leave her alone if you knew what I know.

JUAN. What do you mean? What are you insinuating?

JAIME. I have seen certain things which really . . .

JUAN. Of Carmela? Stupid! *(Someone knocks at the door.)*

JAIME. You open. *(Juan, marches full of indignation toward Jaime, then mechanically goes to the rear door, but stops and turns, about to say something. Colmenero enters from the rear. Evidently he has not waited for the door to be opened. He is received with usual displeasure.)*

COLMENERO. I don't have time to waste waiting at the door. May one see the president of the Chamber of Deputies?

JUAN. No.

COLMENERO. This is the fourth time I've come up.

JUAN. And it's the fourth time I've told you he's taking a bath.

COLMENERO. Come now, man! You know what I usually do when . . . the honorable presidents . . . do not submit a copy of the speeches they are about to deliver when being honored. Read *The Voice* tomorrow.

JUAN. *(Stopping him.)* No, no, don't you make up a speech of your own accord. Really, he is getting dressed. This fellow *(Meaning Jaime.)* also awaits him. Isn't it so, that you are waiting for him to dictate to you?

COLMENERO. Dictate? Now? But it is after eight o'clock . . . All the people are gathered down below, they are impatient . . .

JAIME. Let them wait!

COLMENERO. Starving?

JAIME. *(Arising.)* What do those capitalists know of hunger!

COLMENERO. I have just seen the president of the Bankers' Association eat half a can of caviar . . . and what do you say of the treasurer of the Society for the Protection of Plantation Owners . . . I'll put him against any proletarian when it comes to eating olives . . . *(Buenaventura Padilla comes out all dressed up for the banquet.)* Don Buena! *(After a yank given by Juan he corrects himself.)* Honorable president of the Chamber of Deputies. *(Buenaventura moves himself to accommodate his suit. He stands on the tips of his toes to make his shoes flexible, pulls his collar in order to facilitate breathing.)* Ah! How elegant!

BUENAVENTURA. *(Resigned to feel happy at all costs.)* I'll be darned! Twenty years of struggle for . . . *(Points to his suit.)* for this . . . *(To Juan, returning to his room:)* Look, I'm not going to that banquet dressed like a monkey.

JUAN. *(Holding him back.)* Please wait! *(He tries to fix his tie although Buenaventura slaps his hands.)* You forget who you are.

BUENAVENTURA. Who I am? Me? Come now, man, have I forgotten?

JUAN. You have forgotten.

BUENAVENTURA. Me? *(To Colmenero:)* I am Buenaventura Padilla, isn't that so?

JUAN. Error! You are mistaken.

BUENAVENTURA. Me, mistaken?

COLMENERO. That's right. Buenaventura Padilla is dead.

BUENAVENTURA. Eh?

COLMENERO. He has been buried. They put a carload of dirt over him and have forgotten all about him. *(He drops into a chair and lights a cigarette.)*

BUENAVENTURA. Eh?

JUAN. Now you are the Excellent Honorable President of the Chamber of Deputies. *(Pointing to his abdomen with critical air.)* Look, man . . .

BUENAVENTURA. What's the matter with my albumen? . . .

JUAN. *(Straightening him.)* Head up, up . . . The albumen . . . in . . . like that majestically . . .

BUENAVENTURA. *(Complaining about the position.)* It can't be. This gives me rearitis.

COLMENERO. Rearitis?

BUENAVENTURA. Yes, I feel as if I had weights on my rear. *(Full of fear upon seeing Juan remove the flower from his buttonhole and come toward him to put it in his.)* No! That I'll not allow! I'll dictate . . . dictate . . . Jaime . . . *(Jaime in a bad mood takes the notebook from the table.)* But how am I going to dictate looking at that face? For some time now you have been . . . *(Suddenly.)* What I'd like to know is who took that typewriter I had at the club . . . Juan, do you remember? Ah, how well that machine placed the accents! Tac! An exact accent over the *h*. That machine inspired me . . . inspired me! Juan, take notes as I'm going to give forth a thought on inspiration. The inspiration is called . . . *(Telephone rings.)*

COLMENERO. *(Rising, says to Buenaventura:)* They're calling, calling, calling. *(Taking the phone quickly before Juan.)* Alo? Alo?

JUAN. *(Furious at Colmenero's freshness.)* Have you ever seen!

BUENAVENTURA. You can't expect an oven to produce pears . . .

JUAN. *(To Colmenero:)* Tell them no . . .

COLMENERO. *(While Juan approves and Buenaventura doesn't seem to understand.)* No, no, no . . . no, no . . . no . . .

BUENAVENTURA. I'll confess that I'm intelligent, but . . . I don't understand.

JUAN. People who want to see you . . . *(Colmenero nods.)* The president of such and such a society, this or that millionaire . . . and now we don't have time to see them. The only answer is no . . . no, no . . . no, no . . .

BUENAVENTURA. *(Sitting to remove a shoe which has been annoying him.)* Yes, I have to dictate the speech I'm going to improvise at the banquet.

COLMENERO. These were asking something else.

JUAN. Eh?

COLMENERO. If it would be of any inconvenience for them to come up and greet His Excellency, the president. And I said no, that it would be no inconvenience at all.

JUAN. *(Starting to the back.)* I'll have them stopped. Who were they?

COLMENERO. I believe they told me the general administrator of the government homes for the aged and the new director of the conservatory of music . . .

BUENAVENTURA. Good people! Let them come. It's been a long time since I touched the palm of their hands.

COLMENERO. But they must let you work on your speech. I'll go down and return later. *(As he is going out.)* And tell that watchdog that you have in the hall not to bother me the next time when I want to pass . . .

BUENAVENTURA. Watchdog?

COLMENERO. Yes, that fellow Tirado . . . *(Calling from the hall:)* Eh, Tirado! *(To Buenaventura:)* You have to tell him to let me pass freely. *(To Tirado, who has not as yet appeared:)* You're to come here *(To himself as he returns to the room:)* because you have me plenty annoyed.

BUENAVENTURA. *(Playing with his bare foot.)* Some brave newspaperman who is afraid of a . . . *(He raises his eyes and sees Tirado who has just appeared in the hall.)* You! *(Frightened, he tries to run with his shoe in hand.)*

JUAN. It's Tirado, don't you remember him? *(Shows the scar on his head.)*

BUENAVENTURA. Do I . . .! But . . . that is to say . . . this Tirado!

TIRADO. *(Who has come into the room.)* Mr. President! Your humble servant, Mr. President! The most trustworthy man you could have at your disposal.

JUAN. I asked the chief of police to assign him to your service.

BUENAVENTURA. You! It seems as if you think you have to put a drop in Flanders . . . But . . . But . . . *(He points to the scar on Juan's head.)*

JUAN. Just imagine the clubbings our opponents are going to get . . . Eh, Tirado?

TIRADO. At His Excellency's disposal . . . Whatever the honorable president orders . . .

JUAN. Yesterday he came to me for a recommendation from you for a raise in position. I wrote it myself. And you . . . with the other correspondence signed it.

BUENAVENTURA. I? Twenty years fighting for redemption for this . . . Me! *(Entering from the left the Bugler, who is now director of the conservatory, and the Blind Man, who is now administrator of the homes for the aged, both in full regalia for the banquet.*

The Administrator has smoked glasses on. The Director tries to copy Don Ramón's gestures in his entrance, which is an imitation of Don Ramón's entrance to the club in the first act. At other times, remembering his new position, he waves his cane like a baton.)

DIRECTOR. *(Saluting from the hall after hitting the floor with his cane and coughing.)* President! *(To the others present:)* The new director of the conservatory.

ADMINISTRATOR. *(Going to hug Buenaventura.)* My friend! *(Sliding by Tirado.)* My friend! *(Looks back and gives a jump upon recognizing Tirado. The Director has done the same simultaneously. Juan tries to calm them by indicating to Tirado to leave.)*

JUAN. *(Getting ahead of Colmenero, just as Tirado is about to leave.)* Yes, Tirado, let Colmenero in. *(Tirado leaves left. The Administrator goes as far as the hall to make sure he has gone, then again adopts the airs with which he arrived.)*

ADMINISTRATOR. *(Repeating his race to hug Buenaventura as if nothing had happened.)* My friend! This is the most brilliant homage which could be tributed to any man. I have obliged the doctors of the homes to attend, on the threat of their discharge if they did not come spontaneously. Ah, but you merit it! So many people below! And what people! And so many lights! *(He removes the black glasses.)* No, I couldn't stand so much light. *(Jaime, without hiding his displeasure, turns his back on him and, going to the extreme, sits.)*

COLMENERO. After playing the part of a blind man along the streets, one's sight does become impaired . . .

ADMINISTRATOR. *(Indignant.)* Mr. Newspaperman. Surely you're not saying that because of me, no? *(Buenaventura is stupefied.)*

COLMENERO. *(Ironically.)* Oh, no! Of course not! Isn't it so . . . Mr. Virtue . . . of the . . . *(With a gesture indicates the Bugler.)*

DIRECTOR. *(Repeats the cough and all other guttural noises that he has been emitting since he arrived to make himself important and then for a moment tries to be very modest.)* Director of the conservatory. *(Pointing to the other one.)* Administrator of the homes for the aged. *(The Administrator, who just sat down, gets up, takes a bow, and sits again.)*

COLMENERO. *(Laughing at the spectacle.)* What a pity that I must make use of my time! *(To Buenaventura:)* I'll go down and return later. Let's see if that watchdog dressed up like a sergeant doesn't bother me! *(Goes out left.)*

BUENAVENTURA. *(Thoughtful.)* Watchdog? *(With pity.)* Poor Tirado! Who would have guessed, when he has such good color.

JUAN. *(Hopelessly.)* Please, Ventura!

DIRECTOR. *(To Jaime:)* And you, what's on your mind . . . that you look out of . . . *(Thinking he is making known his musical knowledge)* tune?

JUAN. That's the way he has been lately . . . Bilious! *(Juan and the Director sit.)*

BUENAVENTURA. Just a moment! Jaime is a man of ideas . . . a man of ideals . . . That's why he is my secretary! Secretary to a man like myself can't be any ignoramus . . . and when one has ideas . . . when one has ideals . . . and *(Looking around him.)* one sees certain things . . .

JUAN. Ah, you also have noticed? Jaime, he also . . . *(To Buenaventura:)* Are you sure of what you say?

JAIME. Quiet, man, quiet . . .

ADMINISTRATOR. *(Adjusting his glasses.)* I'd have to be told what there is to be seen . . . *(Knocks heard at the door.)*

DIRECTOR. *(With air of superiority tells Jaime to open the door.)* Jaime, the door . . .

JAIME. *(Without moving causes a commotion between the Director and Administrator.)* Surely some other intruder. Let him stay out! *(A bellboy enters left with a tray filled with telegrams which Juan rises to receive.)*

BELLBOY. More telegrams for Don Buena . . .

DIRECTOR. Don Buena! Fresh! What are we coming to? Isn't there any class distinction anymore?

JUAN. *(Correcting the Bellboy kindly.)* Honorable Mr. President. *(To the others as he turns the telegrams out on the table:)* So many telegrams arrive that I have given orders for them to be brought to me by the hundreds . . . *(Places a coin on the tray.)* or the tips would ruin me.

ADMINISTRATOR. *(Arises. To the Bellboy:)* Wait. *(Takes the tip away from him and returns it to Juan.)* That is a free service given by the hotel. We'll not start any bad habits. *(Reseats himself.)*

DIRECTOR. *(To the Bellboy as he is about to leave:)* The next time do not enter until permission has been granted. Do you by any chance think we are equals? *(Bellboy leaves left.)* Oh democracy!

BUENAVENTURA. *(Having difficulty controlling his fury.)* As I was saying . . . and again repeat . . . one sees certain things . . .

JUAN. Ah, we were coming to that! *(Mysteriously.)* Certain things . . . this one *(Pointing to Jaime.)* also says he has seen . . .

BUENAVENTURA. I am a man who has dedicated his life to the laborious labor of laboring for fraternity, liberty, equality . . . *(Arises and walks toward the back with his shoes in hand.)* Fraternity, liberty, equality: *(Turning.)* There you have my three horns. Twenty years advancing, day by day, stone by stone, with my nails, pursuing in the midst of the tempestuous sea the distant horse of triumph . . . *(To Juan:)* Make notes, Juan, make notes . . . *(Juan brings out his notebook and makes notes.)* Twenty years fighting against privileges, monopolies, egotism, abuses, like Termopilas pursuing the four horsemen of the Epoca Lisa* . . . and now I look around . . . *(The Director and Administrator swell out to be looked upon.)* I look . . . *(Hesitates.)* I look . . . *(Closes his eyes.)* No . . . *(Defrauding.)* I see nothing . . .

JUAN. Nothing? How come nothing? This is a serious case. We have to get together. You must say what you have seen.

BUENAVENTURA. Do you wish it? Do you wish to hear sound the thunder of my verb?

JUAN. For the good of . . .

JAIME. *(Jumping up.)* Quiet? Quiet? *(After a tense moment which follows, the telephone rings.)*

DIRECTOR. *(Answering.)* Who is it? Just a moment . . . *(To Buenaventura:)* It's Miss Concepción Roses . . .

JUAN. *(Answering Buenaventura's silent question.)* She is that humble . . . good . . . virtuous girl . . . daughter of the agitator for Garbanzo . . . You know Concha . . . You put her to work as a stenographer in the chamber . . .

BUENAVENTURA. Stenographer? Magnificent! I'll dictate to her. *(Gives his shoes to Juan, unbuttons his vest which he can no longer stand, and sits down.)*

DIRECTOR. *(Into telephone.)* Please come right up.

JUAN. *(Trying to put the shoes on him.)* Ventura . . . Please . . .

BUENAVENTURA. *(Shaking his feet in order to avoid the shoes.)* With the mood this one's in . . . who can dictate to him? And let's see, why the bad humor? What's the matter? What is it you have to keep . . . from me?

---

*Buenaventura is confusing a famous place-name in Greek military history with biblical figures in Revelation.

JUAN. But you also have not noticed? Didn't you say you had noticed? Then . . . you haven't noticed anything? I knew it. It had to be this one's lies.

BUENAVENTURA. Juan, I'll admit that I have extraordinary intelligence . . . I discover everything, penetrate everything . . . but . . . what's all this about? *(Pause.)* What's it all about? *(Knocks at the door.)*

DIRECTOR. The stenographer!

ADMINISTRATOR. The stenographer! Ah! *(Hurries out left to open the door.)*

DIRECTOR. *(Furious because the Administrator beat him to it.)* But . . . but . . . This man . . . It is . . .

ADMINISTRATOR. *(Reentering, sarcastic and furious at the Director.)* Stenographer! *(Enters the cause of his rage in the form of a Bellboy with a letter on a tray. Juan gestures to take a tip from his pocket, but the Administrator stops him.)* No, not that, let him learn the science of economy. *(Frowning.)* That's the limit! I was going to open the door for a servant! *(To the Director, recriminating:)* Stenographer!

BELLBOY. *(To Juan who takes the letter:)* I was told to await a reply . . .

JUAN. *(To Buenaventura, after reading the address:)* For you. *(Gives it to him.)*

BUENAVENTURA. *(Opens the letter and glances at the signature.)* Ah! *(Crumbling it in his fist.)* From Don Ramón Torres . . . *(The Director marks the importance of the matter with a whistle. Jaime is surprised. Juan grabs the letter from Buenaventura to check the signature.)* It's his signature.

JUAN. Authentic! *(Returns the letter to Buenaventura.)*

BUENAVENTURA. Just a moment! Is that his signature or is that not his signature?

JUAN. Yes, yes. What does he say?

BUENAVENTURA. *(To Jaime, when he was just about to read it himself:)* You read it to us.

JAIME. It says here . . . *(Concepción enters left, very coquettish, resplendent in luxury, transformed into such a grand lady—naturally a version of her native section the Garbanzo—that Buenaventura immediately begins all confused to put on his shoes at the same time as he tries to button his vest. Jaime goes to the back and, sitting, continues to read the letter to himself with growing surprise.)*

CONCEPCIÓN. *(To Bellboy:)* You may go. *(Turning.)* You were the one who brought the letter, no? Yes, you may go. *(Bellboy hesitates, leaves left.)* Hello, hello, Don Buena!

JUAN. *(Almost to himself, correcting with disgust.)* Mr. President . . .

CONCEPCIÓN. *(Looks at Juan, does not understand, continues.)* This Don Buena is so good! *(Using all her coquetry.)* Oowee, but now serious! It seems as if you don't remember me . . . Concepción the stenographer . . . You appointed me stenographer in the chamber . . . by recommendation of Don Juan. Yes, he smiles. *(Buenaventura really continues in the struggle with his shoes and vest, which has now extended to his whole suit.)* And I'm going to make a bet with you. You wouldn't dare refuse what I am going to ask of you? Isn't that so? Granted? Let me help you with those buttons . . . *(Buttons his vest.)* But weren't you going to smile?

DIRECTOR. *(Who has been drooling.)* I'm smiling . . .

ADMINISTRATOR. *(Also drooling.)* Me too . . .

BUENAVENTURA. What is the meaning of ordering people out of here?

CONCEPCIÓN. Precisely regarding that I was going to tell you . . .

BUENAVENTURA. *(Interrupting.)* I have called you because . . . because look at that one's face . . . *(Points to Jaime who, rereading the letter, has made a gesture of fury.)* I must dictate a speech.

CONCEPCIÓN. To me?

BUENAVENTURA. Yes. Take a notebook.

CONCEPCIÓN. Impossible!

ADMINISTRATOR. Oh, God! You're not going to make that little angel work . . .

CONCEPCIÓN. It's that . . . it's that I don't know stenography.

DIRECTOR. How cute she says it!

BUENAVENTURA. And what they dictate to you in the chamber? Why don't you take the dictatorium?

ADMINISTRATOR. Man, she writes it little by little . . . word for word . . .

CONCEPCIÓN. The truth of the matter is I don't know how to write . . .

BUENAVENTURA. Recommended by . . . Don Juan! *(Juan would like to disappear.)*

CONCEPCIÓN. You're not going to refuse me a favor because of that, are you? When you are so generous! I was in Don Ramón's room . . . *(The Director whistles maliciously.)*

BUENAVENTURA. *(To the Director:)* Eh?

DIRECTOR. Nothing, that . . . *(Repeats the whistle but gradually goes into "The Blue Danube.")*

BUENAVENTURA. Ah! "The Blue Vesuvius" . . .

CONCEPCIÓN. I was in his room . . .

BUENAVENTURA. *(Casually.)* Ah, yes? *(Realizing of a sudden.)* Eh?

CONCEPCIÓN. *(While Buenaventura is indignant, he removes his handkerchief from his pocket, opens it, shakes it, refolds it, and replaces it in the pocket a different way.)* That is, first we were downstairs . . . He invited me up to his room for a cocktail . . . and talking, talking . . . he told me of a small farm he has to spend his Sundays far from the world . . . Villa Fortune . . . It's called Villa Fortune. He wants me to go see it. *(The Director chokes from coughing.)* He has such a nice way of making conversation . . .

ADMINISTRATOR. No more than mine!

DIRECTOR. Nor mine! *(Priding himself.)* I know some stories!

CONCEPCIÓN. I say, talking, talking with me. He called you three times on the phone here . . . and lately he didn't even get an answer . . . That's why he decided to write you. Because he says he must see you urgently. And as I'm a friend of you both . . . so I bade him farewell and, without telling him, I decided to come myself . . . because you won't refuse me. You're going to grant me this, aren't you? You'll speak to him? *(Smooths the handkerchief.)* Like that, it's finished . . . Did you read the letter he sent you?

JAIME. *(To Buenaventura:)* You will permit me to interfere . . . *(To Concepción:)* Tell Don Ramón to come without fail . . . right away.

CONCEPCIÓN. *(While Buenaventura is still spellbound.)* I'll go, no? Running, running. *(When she is about to leave, stops.)* No, this merits a prize. *(Takes a flower from the vase, kisses it, and places it in Buenaventura's buttonhole, who is just about able to control his tendency to commit homicide.)* Ah! How elegant! I'll go running, running. *(Leaves very slowly left. The Director and the Administrator follow as far as the hall. Then go to the vase, take a flower, and, each with one in hand, they go rapidly after her.)*

DIRECTOR AND ADMINISTRATOR. *(From the hall:)* Until later, until later . . . *(Leave left.)*

BUENAVENTURA. *(Pulls the flower from his buttonhole and throws it.)* Brr . . . *(To Jaime:)* I don't try to hide from anyone that I am a man of extraordinary intelligence . . . *(Pushes the handkerchief made into a ball into his pocket.)* Brr . . . *(To Jaime:)* But . . . what is the meaning of this receiving Don Ramón? And this "quiet" of a moment ago? *(Peñita, half-dressed, enters left. Tirado evidently is not sure if Peñita is a man to be trusted as he follows him just in case.)*

JUAN. It's alright, Tirado; this one may enter. *(Tirado leaves.)*

PEÑITA. *(Referring to Tirado.)* What a jerky guy. He can't believe that I am a personality like I am. Unless my . . . *(Points to his incomplete clothing as the only possible reason for Tirado's attitude.)* Anyway, the best thing would be to dismiss him. *(Explaining again in a good humor.)* My room is next door, here. Now as I was dressing I got a shock. When I opened my suitcase, I found that . . .

BUENAVENTURA. I imagine, Peñita . . .

PEÑITA. Peña . . . Mr. Peña . . .

BUENAVENTURA. You've found you're without your coat.

PEÑITA. *(Nods.)* I'll not be able to attend the banquet. That's why I've come to present my excuses.

BUENAVENTURA. How about the one you are wearing?

PEÑITA. A man of my position! Secretary of public works, badly dressed at a banquet! What do you think I am? *(Buenaventura makes a motion to remove his coat.)* No . . . no . . . impossible!

BUENAVENTURA. It wouldn't be the first time . . .

PEÑITA. *(Pretending good humor.)* What a joker, eh? I am leaving. I am leaving. Until later. *(Having had it in mind all the time.)* Ah, I almost forgot! How is the speech coming? Did you prepare it already? No? Well, I'm going to give you an idea.

Don't forget to include the paragraph announcing that the project for daylight saving time will be defeated.

BUENAVENTURA. What? The one that permits the industrial slaves a few hours in the afternoon in the sun?

PEÑITA. Really, it's a very pretty project . . .

BUENAVENTURA. Pretty? Pluperfect!

PEÑITA. The only objection is that if we make use of the advantage of one more hour of sun, less electric light will be used at night . . . You can understand that Don Facundo, the president of the Electric Light & Power Company . . . As a summary, Don Facundo has visited me . . . and as you can understand that . . . No? You understand . . . You can't have all the world against you.

BUENAVENTURA. Listen, Peñita . . . Do you remember when you used to take my best suit? *(Gesture of surprise and irresolution by Peñita.)* Remember when you used to go hungry? *(Indignation from Peñita.)* I am merely proving that you have a memory. Do you remember when you had shame, Peñita?

PEÑITA. Eh? Eh? You do not demonstrate any political vision. You'll end up by ruining the party. Until later. And I'm not Peñita. I am Peña. *(Leaves furious, left.)*

BUENAVENTURA. *(Is going to say something so awful that he keeps quiet.)* Jaime . . . Jaime . . . We were talking . . . of what were we talking? *(Muttering.)* Me ruin the party!

JAIME. *(Mysteriously, stands by Buenaventura.)* This letter . . . Take it. Read it. *(Juan draws near, curious.)*

BUENAVENTURA. *(Without taking it.)* A threat? Does Don Ramón also tell me that I'm going to ruin the party?

JAIME. It is composed as if . . . The phraseology seems to indicate . . . If this letter should fall into the hands of an ill-intentioned person . . . of a . . .

BUENAVENTURA. Get on! You mean to say that if it fell into the hands of some worm as God orders . . . a Peñita . . .

JAIME. Exactly. If this letter should fall into the hands of some good-for-nothing . . .

BUENAVENTURA. *(Getting up and walking.)* It would be the same as if a decent person had it. Bah! That leaves me unpreterite. I thought it was something else. Of my life no one can make any discredit or instrumentation. You forget who I am.

JUAN. The president of the Chamber of Deputies!

BUENAVENTURA. No! Buenaventura Padilla! *(One shoe is pinching him, shortens his pleasure. Carmela enters right, dressed for the banquet and very happy.)* Ah! How lovely my little daughter. I didn't think you were ready yet.

CARMELA. *(Coming down into the living room.)* Me! I have been waiting for an hour in my room. You ready at last? Let me look at you. Eh, that tie! *(Straightens it.)* And the handkerchief? *(Takes it out to fix it.)* And the speech? *(Referring to Jaime, whose face has become a mass of wrinkles upon seeing her.)* Ow, what a face! Today you are worse than usual. Do you still have the same thoughts?

JAIME. What's that to you?

BUENAVENTURA. What thoughts?

CARMELA. *(Getting out of the way, confused, spins him around.)* A spin around! Very good! Ah, a button! *(Buttons one on his vest.)*

BUENAVENTURA. I am asking what . . .

CARMELA. Take a few steps . . . *(Buenaventura walks.)* It is clearly noticeable. That left shoe pinches you.

BUENAVENTURA. But . . .

CARMELA. But nothing. What you're doing is wasting time. You haven't prepared the speech, isn't that so? No? You can dictate it to me. *(Replaces the handkerchief in his pocket.)* And your medicine ... Ah, you haven't taken your medicines either! Where are they? There? *(Points to Buenaventura's bedroom.)* Wait ... *(Goes out left door.)*

BUENAVENTURA. It's useless to try to hide things from me ... My intelligence is in all places. My intelligence has the gift of obliquity. Without the smallest indication of any kind, I know that something is the matter here. You, Juan, speak ... *(Juan points to Jaime.)* You, Jaime ... Come out of your shell, or I also will become enshelled.

JAIME. I'd rather not go into this matter on a happy day like today, but if you insist that I do my duty ...

JUAN. If what you say isn't true ...

BUENAVENTURA. Let him make use of words by talking.

JAIME. When the heart is in our ideals, one cannot have the eyes on a bank book ...

BUENAVENTURA. Very well! Because of something you are my pupil pref— *(Stops because of Juan's sour face.)* one of my pupils ...

JAIME. I have caught unawares certain telephone conversations ... I have seen coming and going love letters ...

BUENAVENTURA. Eh?

JAIME. No one will believe in the sincerity of the social ideals of Buenaventura Padilla ...

BUENAVENTURA. What, no?

JAIME. If your daughter is running up and down loose with a capitalist.

BUENAVENTURA. *(To Juan, controlling him:)* Be calm, calm ... *(To Jaime:)* Are you sure?

JAIME. Absolutely.

JUAN. It's a lie!

BUENAVENTURA. Carmela will tell me. You two may go.

JUAN. Without waiting for you?

BUENAVENTURA. You may tell them I'll be right down. After all, they have taken the trouble to come to the homage in my honor with which they are going to honor me. *(Juan throws Jaime's coat at him for him to put on but instead he places it on his arm like a waiter places a napkin.)*

JUAN. We'll take a stroll around in order to calm down the distinguished gentlemen who are waiting below . . . *(Making fun, wanting without much success to appear happy, makes a gesture to protect his billfold.)* Let me protect my billfold as below is the cream of society . . . *(In the hall to Jaime:)* If what you say is a lie . . . *(Goes out left with Jaime. Buenaventura takes a few thoughtful steps to the rear and turns when Carmela enters.)*

CARMELA. *(Enters left with a tray filled with bottles, boxes, glasses, and spoons, which she places on the table.)* Here it is. . . . Today you won't get away from me . . . Which do you want first: the bitter or the sweet? This other, what's it doing here? You've brought the entire cabinet.

BUENAVENTURA. That's the one they gave me when I had the attack, to take by the hour every thirty minutes. But let that go for a minute. *(He sits.)* We have to talk. Jaime has just told me something . . . which really . . .

CARMELA. Jaime! Poor Jaime!

BUENAVENTURA. Poor?

CARMELA. The tormented soul . . . I can imagine what he told you.

BUENAVENTURA. Ah, then it's true! *(Referring to the ringing telephone.)* Again! Say no.

CARMELA. *(Into the phone:)* Yes . . .

BUENAVENTURA. *(Getting up.)* Say no.

CARMELA. *(Into the phone:)* Yes, yes . . . *(Buenaventura starts for the phone.)* Yes, yes . . . *(Hangs up the receiver and turns rapidly to calm Buenaventura.)* It was Concepción to tell you that she has lost your friend in the hotel but that she is trying to locate him.

BUENAVENTURA. My friend? *(With disgust.)* Brr . . . *(Having no other outlet, he kicks the flower he had thrown on the floor and hurts his toe. He sits in another chair.)* Jaime was saying . . .

CARMELA. Father . . . I am madly in love. *(Rapidly goes to his side, puts her arms around him.)* No, no, don't become impatient. I fell in love while I was studying . . . *(Anticipating his question.)* Why hadn't I told you before? *(Walking toward the chair Buenaventura had been using a moment before.)* At first I thought it a dream, a sweet dream of which one cannot speak for fear of awakening . . . *(Turns slowly, rests her back on the back of the chair.)* Afterward, afterward I thought I alone could dominate what I considered madness . . . Well! The madness has gotten stronger than I . . . stronger than you . . . than everything. *(Sits in the chair.)* He has finished at the university. He has taken over his inheritance—left him by his mother, which until now had been administered by his father—and there is no way to get the idea of him marrying me out of his head.

BUENAVENTURA. Ah, what's that, get married! And that fortune that you say he has?

CARMELA. Concerning that . . .

BUENAVENTURA. Five thousand?

CARMELA. Really . . .

BUENAVENTURA. Ten thousand?

CARMELA. There are millions and millions.

BUENAVENTURA. Millions and millions?

CARMELA. What can be done, Father? It's not his fault.

BUENAVENTURA. *(With terror, gets up.)* Millions! Millions! A millionaire in our family! A millionaire in our family, Carmelita! *(Falls in a chair. Phone rings.)* They're going to drive me crazy. I don't want to receive any more silly people.

CARMELA. *(Answers the phone.)* Eh? Oh! Oooh! To see Father? *(To Buenaventura:)* Father, receive one more . . . this one more, no more . . . *(Into the phone, before Buenaventura can stop her:)* Yes, right away. Father says with pleasure . . . *(To Buenaventura:)* This time it is . . .

BUENAVENTURA. *(Furious, goes to the phone.)* Alo . . . alo . . . Disconnect this thing.

CARMELA. Let me explain . . .

BUENAVENTURA. Buenaventura Padilla, father-in-law to a millionaire! I am looking like it already! Look at me. Twenty years of struggle for redemption . . . *(Referring to his suit.)* If the laborers, if the unfortunates who gave us their votes could see the consequences! What would my friends say, the stevedores at the piers, if I go now and ask them to arise in a hunger strike . . . *(Looking at himself.)* A monkey . . . like this?

CARMELA. Father, calm yourself, calm yourself . . . Remember that the doctors have advised you to keep tranquil . . .

BUENAVENTURA. *(Walking.)* Peñita! The one from the conservatory! The Blind Man! Concepción! And the next one and the next and next . . . How triumph spoils! *(Carmela sits in the chair Buenaventura has just left.)* And on top of all the others, you.

My daughter! *(Goes toward her.)* The daughter I wanted to be like that other saint who was killed.

CARMELA. Mother has always been my model.

BUENAVENTURA. That one was proud of me, of Ventura the laborer. You, you . . . your pride is a capitalist. You have compared and chosen.

CARMELA. *(Arising.)* If you'd let me explain . . .

BUENAVENTURA. Why don't you find yourself a man like Jaime?

CARMELA. You're not going to tell me that you believe in class distinction . . . Neither in the high nor the low . . .

BUENAVENTURA. No, no, I don't believe in classes . . . But of one thing I am diamentrically sure: a daughter of mine should at least be a daughter of mine . . . *(Drops into a chair.)*

CARMELA. Father . . . make believe you are twenty years old . . .

BUENAVENTURA. What?

CARMELA. *(Going to him.)* Twenty years old . . . Are you making believe? Think back to when you were twenty. *(Very slowly she takes a turn about Buenaventura.)* Make believe you played a lottery ticket. Yes, yes, make believe. But give me an opportunity for defense. Think. Ready? Now make believe you won the big prize. No, no, no . . . Have you thought of it? Please . . . *(She is able to keep Buenaventura in the chair as he is about to get up.)*

BUENAVENTURA. Don't talk foolishness.

CARMELA. You're rich, very rich . . . You have the big prize. You're twenty years old. And now . . . now you have just seen a girl you like . . . now you see Mother . . .

BUENAVENTURA. *(Getting up.)* But what is this? What are you saying?

CARMELA. Let me finish. Please, Father . . . no, no . . . listen.

BUENAVENTURA. *(Turning.)* What are you trying to do?

CARMELA. I only want you to answer me this: because luck had made you rich, wouldn't you love her just the same? Couldn't you marry her? Would you let the money stop you? Answer. Why don't you answer?

BUENAVENTURA. *(Moving away, head down.)* That is a seamless question.

CARMELA. Just because you had money, would you let her love someone else?

BUENAVENTURA. *(Turning toward her.)* What! Quiet! She, love another! Are you crazy? Carmela, respect . . . your mother was a saint.

CARMELA. Well then?

BUENAVENTURA. No. Let's speak no more of that. Get the notebook.

CARMELA. Without telling me yes or no?

BUENAVENTURA. Get the notebook. The best thing is that I dictate the speech to you. *(A knock at the door. Carmela runs to the hall at the rear.)* No, don't open. Astringent measures must be taken.

CARMELA. Even if only for a minute . . . a few words . . . Just meet him . . . It's the one who phoned a minute ago . . . *(Goes out rapidly left.)*

BUENAVENTURA. *(To Carmela, who has left:)* It's that my head is dancing . . . It's that I have to make that speech . . . *(Carmela enters left with George who is dressed for the banquet and very happy.)*

CARMELA. Father . . . this is . . .

BUENAVENTURA. Yes, yes . . . the one who called . . . *(Getting away from him without knowing or caring who he is.)* How is that family? Very well, eh? Very well. I'm glad. I find you stouter than the last time . . . Oh, yes, yes! Very much in health . . . Will you be so kind as to tell her what you wish . . . because I have to make a speech . . . *(Takes the notebook and pencil from the small table and starts for his bedroom. To Carmela:)* If it's a matter of a letter of recommendation, write it for him and I'll sign it later.

CARMELA. Father . . . Father . . . listen . . .

BUENAVENTURA. *(Almost to himself.)* Now is when I need the typewriter they stole from me at the club. *(Goes out left.)*

GEORGE. *(Sits down, happily.)* Formidable! He almost convinced me that he had seen me before . . . If it weren't for that he said he found me stouter . . . Imagine: with the presidency of some twenty enterprises just fallen on me! Anyway, he left orders for me to tell you what I wish. And what I wish is . . . *(Gets up, nears her to kiss her, but she draws away.)*

CARMELA. Will you get some sense some day? I have just informed him of our relations.

GEORGE. Wonderful! Reaction? Reaction positive! Your eyes can't fool me! Positive! *(Loudly.)* Long live Don Buenaventura Padilla!

CARMELA. For God's sake! Are you crazy?

GEORGE. You're not going to deny that it's positive . . . Look, I may be capable of loving you even more. No, I correct myself. More is impossible.

CARMELA. By what I could conclude . . . judging by what I told him . . . maybe . . .

GEORGE. *(Interrupting.)* That's enough. I have entered the family. *(Taking the phone.)* Alo . . .

CARMELA. What are you going to do?

GEORGE. Order champagne to celebrate this.

CARMELA. *(Nearing him.)* For God's sake, George, you are no longer a student. When are you going to get some sense?

GEORGE. We must celebrate, Carmelita. Obviously you don't know what this means to me!

CARMELA. But, George . . . champagne like that . . . here . . .

GEORGE. Ah! Here, no? Tell them downstairs at the canteen. Let's go. Let's go. A toast to my luck! *(Begging.)* Just one cocktail!

CARMELA. And leave Father at the mercy of the intruders? . . .

GEORGE. Remedied immediately . . . *(In the hall, calling:)* Eh, sergeant! *(To Carmela:)* Let me carry on. For me today no problem can present itself. *(To Tirado, who enters left:)* Sit down here. Get comfortable. *(Makes him comfortable in a chair.)* Fine, now don't let anyone annoy Don Buenaventura. No one! *(Pulling Carmela.)* Let's go, we'll come back. Half a minute . . .

CARMELA. *(Stepping back.)* Wait. *(To Buenaventura through the bedroom door:)* Until later, Father.

GEORGE. Your blessing, Father. *(Both run out left. Tirado, once alone, spreads himself all over the chair, but jumps when Buenaventura enters.)*

BUENAVENTURA. *(Enters left, wearing one shoe and one slipper. The other slipper he carries in his hand.)* You? Really, I don't know why you called me Father, but—God bless you!

TIRADO. Mr. President . . . I . . . believe that . . . through that door . . . To me . . .

BUENAVENTURA. Bah! Don't worry about it. A man in your poor health shouldn't worry . . . What good does it do! Where do you have the cancer?

TIRADO. *(Expressing terror.)* Me? You mean me?

BUENAVENTURA. No? Ah, that Colmenero! I'm glad it's not so, because I'm going to ask a favor of you.

TIRADO. At your command, Mr. President. Do you want me to give a good clubbing to those you don't like below?

BUENAVENTURA. Me, no . . .

TIRADO. Would you prefer a tear bomb during the dessert? Or a killing when they all come out?

BUENAVENTURA. No, something more important: get me the typewriter they stole from me at the club . . . *(When he is going to sit down to put on the slipper, Concepción enters left, followed by Don Ramón who is also dressed for the banquet.)*

CONCEPCIÓN. *(To Don Ramón, while Buenaventura hides the hand with the slipper:)* Here he is . . . here he is . . . *(To Tirado:)* Will you please go out, as these gentlemen have private matters to talk over . . . *(To Don Ramón, with a caress:)* Don't be long, as I'll be waiting for you below . . . Ramón . . . *(Leaves left following Tirado to whom she makes signs for him to go.)*

DON RAMÓN. *(Upon extending his hand to Buenaventura, he almost shakes hands with the slipper he has in his right hand.)* Oh! Oh! *(With his cough of importance, while Buenaventura, not knowing what to do with the slipper, puts it in his pocket.)* Before anything else let me congratulate you for this great homage being paid you. All the live forces are represented. And with sincerity, you merit it; you have won it with your corrupt legislative labor . . .

BUENAVENTURA. *(Trying in vain to hide his pride.)* One does what one can, as Aristotle used to say . . .

DON RAMÓN. Did you read my letter?

BUENAVENTURA. No.

DON RAMÓN. All the better. I'll go into the matter from the beginning. *(Pulls up a chair and sits down.)* Where were we? Ah, your legislation. *(Buenaventura also sits down.)* I have been told that it is on the calendar for tomorrow morning's session of the chamber . . . That's why it was urgent for me to see you . . . Oh, wise, very wise legislation! Naturally, to differ is human; there will always be small differences of criterion . . . But the first virtue of all big government men is to know how to find formulas of harmony . . . reach fruitful understandings . . . Of course, you with that eagle vision with which you are gifted . . .

BUENAVENTURA. You also believe it?

DON RAMÓN. A group of friends, bankers, industrialists, directors of big farming corporations have been discussing the matter . . . and we are all in accord . . . your legislative program is magnificent . . . with some small exceptions . . . easily remedied . . .

BUENAVENTURA. Bah! Schools for the illiterate . . . hospitals and medicines for the sick . . . homes for those who don't have them, farms for the laborers in the country . . . pensions for the old . . . better salaries and insurance against unemployment for the workers . . . bread for the hungry . . . protection for abandoned children . . . Because I never tire of repeating that phrase of mine used so much by orators at school graduations: The child of today is the man of tomorrow. Deep, isn't it? In fact a series of projects from the first to the twenty-fifth . . . Social justice for those who have nothing, and it all comes by merely taxing those who have more than enough.

DON RAMÓN. Precisely . . . That is the small discrepancy. The rest is alright . . . but this last . . .

BUENAVENTURA. *(Explaining a gesture of pain.)* No, nothing . . . It's the shoe.

DON RAMÓN. Isn't there some way to reach one of the productive understandings of which we were speaking?

BUENAVENTURA. I admit that I am intelligent . . . but if you don't explain to me . . .

DON RAMÓN. You are a sick man. Have you looked in the mirror at the circles under your eyes? And your pulse, how is your pulse? Terrible! Horrible! You know it. *(Pointing to what is on the table.)* Medicines! And more medicines! You are very ill! You'll end up by dying. *(Buenaventura, scared, runs to the table where the medicines are, sits down near it, and swallows one of the pills quickly.)*

BUENAVENTURA. Four doctors are caring for me . . .

DON RAMÓN. *(Going to him.)* They remedy nothing. Half a dozen of us, your friends, have gotten together, and we have agreed that you need to see Doctor Foncé at the Sorbonne, and the specialist Schmidt in Berlin . . .

BUENAVENTURA. Go abroad, me? Really, it has been one of the dreams of my life. The sea! My love for the sea has been the inspiration for some of my most beautiful semaphores. But the nearest I have gotten to the sea has been the warehouses at the piers . . . Where am I going to get the money for a trip?

DON RAMÓN. That's what friends are for. We six have agreed to each contribute ten thousand . . . *(Throwing a billfold on the table.)* There you have sixty thousand . . .

BUENAVENTURA. One minute!

DON RAMÓN. You will leave this very week and when you return . . . those projects in which there are small discrepancies . . . will have died.

BUENAVENTURA. *(Arising.)* Now I understand. Sixty thousand dollars for the death of my social projects. Rejecting it, I reciprocate your thanks.

DON RAMÓN. It could be raised to a hundred thousand . . .

BUENAVENTURA. And you tell me this with that prime face! Have you read the book of Don Quijote and Sancho Panza?

DON RAMÓN. Yes.

BUENAVENTURA. Then you know that Don Quijote was a man who walked on clouds . . . a crazy one with a head full of silliness . . . who attacked windmills without benefit . . . A dreamer . . .

DON RAMÓN. Yes, yes . . . While Sancho . . .

BUENAVENTURA. While Sancho was a practical man, a man with five senses, who knew how to defend his interests.

DON RAMÓN. Exactly. You're not given to romanticism . . . No?

BUENAVENTURA. I am Sancho.

DON RAMÓN. Then . . . We're agreed on a hundred thousand?

BUENAVENTURA. Don't you hear what I say? I am Sancho.

DON RAMÓN. More than the hundred thousand?

BUENAVENTURA. You don't have to come to me with dreams or silliness. I am a practical man, in my five senses. That's all I needed! Please get out. Thinking me to be a Quijote!

DON RAMÓN. No, no, Sancho . . . That is to say . . . really . . . I am confused. I'd like to understand you a little better.

BUENAVENTURA. Out, I have said. I am no Quijote.

DON RAMÓN. Decidedly . . . Yours is a life for Plutarch!

BUENAVENTURA. *(Calling from the rear:)* Tirado! Tirado! *(Tirado enters running.)* This man is threatening me with a guy named Plutarch. Get him out of here for me.

TIRADO. *(To Don Ramón:)* Out, insolent! And if anything happens to His Excellency, the president ... *(To Buenaventura when Don Ramón is already in the hall:)* Shall I fire a shot at him outside?

BUENAVENTURA. No! *(To Don Ramón:)* Ah, the billfold! *(To Tirado:)* You take it and give it to him, as I don't want to leave the paraffin of my fingerprints on it.

TIRADO. *(Takes the billfold and goes out left after Don Ramón, at the same time fixing it, and Colmenero enters by the same way.)* Hurry up! Hurry up!

BUENAVENTURA. Quijote, me! That's all I needed.

COLMENERO. *(Taking out his notebook.)* But what's the matter?

BUENAVENTURA. *(Walking up and down excitedly.)* That I am not Quijote. That I don't need any Sorbonne ...

COLMENERO. No?

BUENAVENTURA. I have never believed in windmills. Tell me, have you ever seen me with a lance in its socket? Sixty thousand dollars! ... *(With disgust.)* Brr ...

COLMENERO. Man, remember at least that that is a sum which merits major consideration and respect ...

BUENAVENTURA. Make notes, as I am going to paint the whole body of the face with which that man came here ... I'm going to tell who Don Ramón is ...

COLMENERO. For *The Voice*?

BUENAVENTURA. Naturally, for *The Voice* to sing.

COLMENERO. Well ... really ... Obviously you don't know that all the debts of *The Voice*, which were not few, have been consolidated in one person: Don Ramón Torres. *The Voice* has been taken already. Now then, I believe I heard you say sixty thousand dollars ...

BUENAVENTURA. *(Meditating.)* A hundred thousand . . . The price for the death of my social projects . . .

COLMENERO. Eh? What? Really? A hundred thousand? No, no, tell me no more, because the debts of *The Voice . . . (Almost to himself:)* Ah! But . . . and Don Ramón? If Don Ramón would tell me something . . . I'll ask Don Ramón . . . *(Enter left Juan and Jaime who has at last put on his coat.)*

JUAN. It is impossible to wait any longer. The meat has burned. The guests are fainting.

COLMENERO. And Don Ramón?

JUAN. What do I know of Don Ramón?

COLMENERO. Don Ramón! That's my man! Until later.

BUENAVENTURA. *(Stopping him.)* Don't ask him. Thinking it over . . . I haven't said a word . . . You have heard nothing . . . The best course is silence . . . Silence!

COLMENERO. *(Looking for an excuse.)* Anyway . . . I was leaving . . . *(To Juan:)* You haven't seen him, you say? Until later . . . A hundred thousand dollars! *(Leaves quickly left. Jaime brings from his pocket Don Ramón's letter, looks at it with distrust, and puts it away again.)*

BUENAVENTURA. Juan . . . get out your notebook, as I feel thoughts boiling over . . . *(Nears him.)* I am going to tell you an aneurysm . . . something genial which is forming in my brain. Ready! Note: Silence is . . . Silence is . . .

JUAN. *(Proud to be of help.)* Gold. Silence is gold.

BUENAVENTURA. No! Not gold! Gold is dirty. *(The Bellboy enters left with a tray of telegrams. Juan takes them. Buenaventura, depressed, puts his hand in his pocket and gives all he has to the boy as a tip.)* Here, dirty your hands. *(Amidst the general surprise, he takes one of the telegrams from the tray, which Juan is holding near him, tears the envelope, and throws it, then Juan puts the rest on the table and returns the tray to the Bellboy who goes out left scared. Buenaventura hands the telegram to Juan.)* Read me words from the humble. I think I need it. *(Walks toward the chair in which he is about to sit, distracted in sad thoughts. Juan is about to read the telegram. George and Carmela enter left very happy.)*

CARMELA. Look at him . . . We were celebrating. Isn't it true that he isn't an ogre?

GEORGE. Yes, yes, look at me . . . as you're going to have to see a lot of me from now on . . .

BUENAVENTURA. But who is he?

CARMELA. My sweetheart. Isn't he pleasing? He is George Torres.

GEORGE. George Torres . . . your future son-in-law.

JAIME. Don Ramón's son . . . *(Buenaventura drops into a chair unable to say a word.)* Never, with the Master's consent . . . Isn't that so . . . The Master hasn't put his only daughter up for sale . . . Isn't that so. *(Buenaventura hardly hears him.)* Am I right or am I right? *(Buenaventura moves his lips as if to say something but is unable to.)*

JUAN. *(Holding George back.)* No, no violence in front of the Master. *(Scolding Jaime.)* At a time like this! *(Anticipating his answer.)* Shut up, idiot! *(Wanting to give a cheerful air to the situation.)* It's all over now. Not another word. A fortunate man, this Ventura, Don Buenaventura Padilla, president of the Chamber of Deputies! Pay attention to this. It's signed by about twenty comrades from the piers. *(To Buenaventura, wanting to cheer him:)* Do you remember those good people? Perucho, who had boats? Quique, who was tattooed? They hold you in high esteem. Yes, they do! Listen! *(Reading.)* To the Honorable Buenaventura Padilla, president of the Chamber of Deputies: H, period; E, period . . . *(Intrigued, draws an* H *and* E *in the air.)* Ah, yes! *H. E.* His Excellency! "His Excellency may feel himself today the happiest man on earth . . ."

JAIME. Cut out the messages . . . I want to know the truth, the truth! I want to know if Buenaventura Padilla has also turned capitalist.

CARMELA. *(Throwing herself at his feet.)* Father, Father . . . let me explain . . .

BUENAVENTURA. *(Depressed.)* The happiest man on earth! My Excellency!

CURTAIN

Left to right: Buenaventura Padilla (Benjamín Morales) and Peñita (Félix Antelo). From the 1966 production of *Mi señoría* presented by the Institute of Puerto Rican Culture (Instituto de Cultura Puertorriqueña) at the Tapia Theater in San Juan, Puerto Rico. Photograph courtesy of the Institute of Puerto Rican Culture—General Archives of Puerto Rico.

Third Act Synopsis

Presented here is a synopsis of the third act—the entire Spanish text follows—to provide a summary of its dramatic action and the play's outcome, as Williams's translation has either been lost or, possibly, was never made.* The set is Buenaventura's office in the capitol, described this way in the stage directions:

> Private office of the president of the Chamber of Deputies, with utilitarian decor. At the right, downstage, a door that goes to a waiting room from where one passes through a corridor to the meeting room of the chamber, now assembled; upstage, the only ornament in the office: a large portrait of a humble woman. At the left, downstage, a door that leads to other rooms by the office; upstage, a large glass window that overlooks the street. At the back, a platform with Buenaventura's desk on it. On the wall behind it, stylized and dominant, a shield with the embossed insignia of the Workers Party. Carmela's small table for taking notes, with a telephone. A file cabinet. A few chairs, expensive and uncomfortable.

Buenaventura's office is businesslike, in keeping with his humble character. It is significant that his aides want to change the barebones decor by adding more luxurious furnishings. The room's only decoration is the portrait of Buenaventura's wife, who continues as a motif in this act, now visually instead of only through dialogue. The typewriter, soon restored to Buenaventura, is an effective symbol. It had been with him throughout his political career. He loves his old typewriter. It was both his professional badge and his connection

*All translations from the Spanish script are by the editor. Grateful acknowledgment is made to Jordan Phillips for critical observations described in his work *Contemporary Puerto Rican Drama* (1973).

with learning: his writing machine that had enabled him to broadcast his political message and calls for action. "Ah, my machine!" he tenderly exclaims upon seeing it after its recovery from Don Ramón's thugs. "What articles by me are going to come from it now!"

In the act's opening scene, Juan and Carmela are alone together in the office. He is standing while dictating to her a new law to be created to address what he calls an "urgent situation"; namely, the need to renovate the office. The waiting rooms must be "much more comfortable and elegant." Jaime then enters, and the betrayals of Buenaventura begin to unfold as described below. Carmela, though, is always loyal to her father, but her relationship with George has upset him. This makes it look like he has sold out to Don Ramón. Buenaventura is already suffering from the conflict of the honorary banquet held in a luxurious hotel and from Don Ramón's proposition and threat. Love, then, is addressed in this act on different levels. In a heated moment with Jaime, Buenaventura declares that love is the essential element of his political actions: "For love of the helpless to fight against the powerful, for love of justice to fight the abuse . . . Fires, sabotages, strikes, protests, out of love, not hatred . . . For love!"

The previous act showed that Buenaventura had put himself in a precarious position because of his naivete. His appointment of his friends to government jobs underscores the play's theme of the corrupting power of political victory. Casting a spotlight on three of these appointees, the third act exposes their betrayals. Juan, the ever-faithful friend who had been close with Buenaventura from the very beginning of his struggle for social justice, falls victim to the allure of Don Ramón's money, which he offers him for medical treatment in Europe. Jaime, the young idealist who had been Buenaventura's favorite and his personal secretary, disgusted by the new officials' corruption, now believes that Buenaventura has accepted the same kind of deal from Don Ramón and becomes Buenaventura's accuser and rival. Peñita, who had begged Buenaventura for a suit to give to his brother so that he might vote for him and was then appointed secretary of public works, turns on his benefactor in this act. He boldly confronts Buenaventura and tells him: "You are going down!

The party will have another president within forty-eight hours. Anyone . . . but you."

The third act thus shows Buenaventura losing everything. He is no longer a purely entertaining buffoon but a sad, tragicomic figure. Successfully undermining him toward the end of the act, Don Ramón uses his controlling power over the newspaper *The Voice* to slander him with a destructive front-page story headlined "PRESIDENT OF THE CHAMBER BRIBED. SOLD SOCIAL LEGISLATION FOR FIFTY THOUSAND DOLLARS." The members of his Workers Party then turn against him. At the end, Don Ramón's son George puts him in the curious position of supporting Buenaventura's social reforms. The support comes too late, however, for the defeated president. A full circle is made. Stones thrown by a mob outside, led by his former comrades, break the window of his office. In a delirium caused by his fatigue, disappointment, and the neglect of his health, he recalls the people he championed in the struggle—the workers, the sick, the orphaned, the aged, the imprisoned—in a sentimental moment. He alludes to them in the closing of the play:

GEORGE. I am ready to implement any reform . . . Any.

BUENAVENTURA. *(Without responding to him.)* They are waiting for me . . . Far from all this . . . My immortal talent . . . My work . . . They are waiting for me . . .

CARMELA. You're delirious, Father!

BUENAVENTURA. *(Incoherently.)* In democracy . . . in liberty . . . in sorrow . . . No! . . . I'm strong . . . They won't destroy me . . .

CARMELA. *(Seeing that Buenaventura is about to collapse.)* Father! Father!

BUENAVENTURA. In love . . . in love . . . *(He falls and tumbles down the stairs.)*

CURTAIN

Drawing of the set for the third act by Pedro Luis Tosado, set designer of the 1966 production of *Mi señoría* presented by the Institute of Puerto Rican Culture (Instituto de Cultura Puertorriqueña) at the Tapia Theater in San Juan, Puerto Rico. Courtesy of the Institute of Puerto Rican Culture—General Archives of Puerto Rico.

Acto Tercero

Despacho privado del presidente de la Cámara de Diputados, de líneas romanas. En lateral derecha, en primer término, puerta que comunica con una sala de espera, de donde se pasa por un corredor al salón de sesiones de la Cámara, reunida ahora; en segundo término, el único adorno del despacho: un gran retrato de una humilde mujer. En lateral izquierda, en primer término, una puerta que lleva a otras dependencias de la oficina; en segundo término, una amplia ventana de cristales, que da a la calle. Al fondo, un estrado, sobre el cual se destaca el escritorio de Buenaventura Padilla. En relieve, en la pared, estilizado y dominante, un escudo con la insignia del Partido Obrero. Mesita de Carmela tomar notas, con teléfono. Un archivo. Pocas sillas, caras e incómodas. JUAN, *de pie, está dictando a* CARMELA.

JUAN. "Se declara por la presente que existe una situación de urgencia, por lo cual esta ley empezará a regir inmediatamente después de su aprobación . . ." ¿Está? ¡Bien! Ahora te voy a dictar el proyecto para dotar las bartolinas con saloncitos de espera. Por supuesto, saloncitos mucho más cómodos y elegantes que este maldito despacho privado del presidente de la Cámara . . . *(Mirando alrededor.)* Después de uno haber estado anoche en aquel hotel del banquete es que comprende que aquí no hay gusto. *(Señalando el estrado.)* Mira qué mamarracho . . . Yo no sé cómo tu padre consintió que le pusieran su escritorio ahí encima.

CARMELA. ¿Fue Peñita el de la idea, no?

JUAN. Sí, Peñita. Decía él que un hombre de los méritos de Ventura no podía tener su escritorio pegado al suelo como el resto de la humanidad. En fin, desde ese punto de vista no está mal . . . *(Se queda un momento pensativo.)* ¿Qué comisión se llevaría el empleado que se encargó de la compra de estos muebles? *(Reanudando su dictado.)* Proyecto de ley . . .

CARMELA. Descansemos.

JUAN. ¡Oh, no! *(Dicta paseándose.)* Proyecto de ley de la Cámara . . . número tal tal . . . del diputado tal tal . . . para dotar las bartolinas . . . ¿Qué? ¿No escribes?

CARMELA. Estoy tan cansada . . .

JUAN. Yo sé lo que tú quieres. ¡Y no!

CARMELA. ¿No me vas a dejar respirar?

JUAN. Mira, Carmelita, a mí no me engañas . . . Conque . . . *(Dictando.)* Proyecto de ley de la Cámara número tal tal . . . *(Notando que ella no escribe.)* ¡Eso es lo que tú quieres! Divagar, torturarte, pensar en lo de anoche. Te olvidas porque te olvidas del asunto. Prosigamos. *(Dictando.)* Proyecto de ley de . . . *(Sentándose cerca de ella al notar que no escribe.)* ¿Pero no ves que lo que quiero es ayudarte? Ahí afuera, en esa Cámara, hay esta tarde un ambiente raro, algo extraño que yo quisiera investigar, porque no sé, ojalá me equivoque—me parece que Ventura necesita de mí hoy más que nunca; y sin embargo aquí me estoy encerrado en su despacho . . . dictando . . . dictando cuanto se me ocurre, nada más que por mantenerte alejada de tus pensamientos. Y tú . . . sin cooperar conmigo . . . ¡Que estás cansada! . . . *(Levantándose.)* ¡Oh, no, tú no te sales con la tuya! Vamos. *(Dictando.)* Proyecto de ley número tal tal . . . *(A ella se le aguan los ojos.)* Está bien. Me doy por vencido. Ganaste. Piensa todo lo que te parezca. Mortifícate con ese amor desgraciado.

CARMELA. No puedo dejar de pensar en papá. Ya lo viste hace un rato cuando salía a presidir la sesión. No me permitió hablarle del asunto. Así está desde anoche. ¡Si él me diera una oportunidad de explicarle!

JUAN. ¿Para qué? Si quieres ese muchacho, eso es una desgracia, pero allá tú. Ventura ama demasiado la libertad de cada cual para meterse en eso. Ya tú habrás notado a Jaime también . . .

CARMELA. Con su ceño . . . su adustez . . .

JUAN. Sí, que está que no hay quien le beba el caldo porque tu padre no ha querido decir ni que sí ni que no a este asunto . . .

CARMELA. *(Levantándose y acercándose a Juan.)* ¡Si tú quisieras explicarle a papá! . . .

JUAN. ¿Yo?

CARMELA. Te contaré y tú . . .

JUAN. ¿Yo?

CARMELA. Tú podrías . . .

JUAN. ¿Yo? No. Yo no. No trates de convencerme a mí. Yo caigo siempre con el Maestro. *(Con gran interés, a Jaime que entra por la derecha.)* ¿Algo de nuevo? ¿No ha pasado nada? Porque me pareció notar un ambiente ahí afuera . . .

JAIME. ¿Ah, sí?

JUAN. Espera . . .

JAIME. Voy a buscar unos papeles. Vuelvo.

JUAN. Pero tú sabes algo, ¿eh?

JAIME. ¿Sí? *(Sale izquierda.)*

JUAN. ¿Has notado ese tono . . . esa manera como de serpiente?

CARMELA. ¡Ni me ha mirado! ¡Pobre Jaime!

JUAN. ¿Por qué te desprecia?

CARMELA. Porque me ama . . .

JUAN. ¿Eh? ¡Pamplinas! *(De la sala de sesiones llegan aplausos y silbidos.)*

CARMELA. Parece que hay debate en la Cámara . . .

JUAN. ¿Jaime amarte, dijiste? *(Con desprecio, por Jaime.)* ¡Bah!

CARMELA. ¡Me produce una pena tan grande no poder quererlo! *(De la sala de sesiones llega otra ola de aplausos, silbidos y gritos contradictorios: "¡No!" "¡Bien!" "¡Abajo!" Jaime entra por la izquierda con unos papeles en la mano, a los cuales da una última ojeada antes de guardárselos en el bolsillo, y va a buscar otros al archivo.)*

JUAN. *(A Jaime, por los aplausos y silbidos:)* ¿Qué es eso?

JAIME. Discurso de don Buenaventura . . .

JUAN. *(Alarmadísimo.)* ¡Eh! ¡Qué! ¿Con esas protestas? *(Queriendo imitar la indiferencia de Jaime.)* ¿Ah, sí? *(Arrecia el alboroto afuera, y la indiferencia afectada de Juan se viene al suelo.)* ¡Ventura! ¡Silbado! *(Sale apresuradamente por la derecha.)*

CARMELA. *(Deteniendo a Jaime que va a salir impasible.)* Jaime . . . perdóname por todo el mal que te he hecho.

JAIME. ¿A mí? Ninguno.

CARMELA. Sí, ya no eres el mismo. Sin quererlo he puesto hiel en tu corazón . . .

JAIME. Te equivocas. Te estoy agradecido. Tú me has hecho un hombre.

CARMELA. ¿Porque el cielo no me escuchó mi ruego de que me hiciera amarte?

JAIME. Porque he comprendido mejor este miserable barro humano. Es verdad: te quería. Ahora . . . ahora . . . te conozco.

CARMELA. ¿Me olvidarás entonces? ¿Serás feliz sin mí?

JAIME. ¡Bah! ¿Qué eres tú? Otra mujer más. Otra más que se vende. Ni siquiera esa originalidad has tenido: todas se venden. Todas están en pública subasta . . . ¡A la una! ¡A las dos! ¿Qué se me ofrece por esta mujer encantadora? "Mi apellido y mis corbatas," contesta un zángano social. "Mis músculos," clama un atleta. "Mi fortuna," grita un burgués. ¡Y el pobre Jaime, el buenazo de Jaime, tiene que callar! A codazos lo sacan de la rueda de licitadores. Un triste secretario no puede ofrecer más que ideales, que no se cotizan; no puede ofrecer más que amor, *(Yendo a ella, exaltado.)* esa ridícula baratija que se llama amor. ¡Amor! ¿Recuerdas la palabra? Algo *(Dándole la espalda.)* que sólo existe en la mente de los cándidos.

CARMELA. ¡Pobre Jaime, cuánto me amas!

JAIME. *(Volviéndose.)* ¿Estás loca? ¿Amarte? No, ahora vas a verme en la subasta, en las subastas. ¿Qué se ofrece por esta rubia divina? ¿Por esta trigueña? ¿Por esos ojos? ¿Por estos labios inocentes que jamás fueron besados? Vas a oír a mi voz responder: un partido que me sigue, las prebendas del poder repartidas a mi antojo, el país entero sometido a mi dictadura, la gloria de los vencedores . . . Vas a ver mis compras, fáciles y múltiples . . .

CARMELA. Has perdido el sentido.

JAIME. Se acabó el secretario devoto y anónimo . . . Aquí, aquí *(Subiendo hasta el escritorio de Buenaventura.)* he de sentarme yo. Si tu padre es el jefe, el dueño del país, ¿por qué no lo puedo ser yo?

JUAN. *(Que entra por la derecha escucha las últimas palabras.)* Porque eres un imbécil . . . Y eres un traidor . . . *(Llegan de la sala aplausos, silbidos, gritos.)* ¿Oyes? Eso es una conjura. Y tú estás en ella.

CARMELA. ¿Qué discuten?

JUAN. Otro de los proyectos que traen disgustado a Peñita: el que impide que la Compañía de la Luz Eléctrica siga estafando al público.

CARMELA. Me pareció oír aplausos.

JUAN. De las galerías. La Cámara entera silba a Ventura. Menos mal que Tirado ha tomado las debidas precauciones. *(A Jaime:)* Tú estás en el complot.

CARMELA. ¿Jaime? ¡No! No digas disparates, padrino Juan . . . ¡Jaime, no!

JUAN. Acaban de asegurarme que se ha pasado el día murmurando de Ventura. *(A Jaime:)* A esto nada más he venido: a saber qué es lo que tienes que alegar . . . Habla, que necesito volverme al lado de Ventura.

JAIME. Yo no niego mis actos. ¡Es cierto! Creía a Buenaventura Padilla un apóstol. Me equivoqué. Es un hombre sin ninguna sinceridad en la doctrina social que predica. Se lo he dicho a todo el que ha querido oírme: que es un burgués disfrazado. Peor . . . Que es un traficante de nuestros ideales . . .

CARMELA. *(Interponiéndose.)* No, padrino Juan. ¡Déjalo! ¡Déjalo! Hasta esos límites de locura es capaz de llegar el amor.

JAIME. Eso les he dicho; y les he dicho más . . . *(Bajando del estrado.)* Les he dicho la terrible razón de mis palabras . . . , les he dicho por qué lo he dicho.

JUAN. ¡Por qué! ¡Por qué! ¿Pero, por qué? ¿Qué insinúa este hombre? Carmela, salte un momento de aquí . . .

CARMELA. *(Reprochándolo.)* ¡Pero, padrino Juan!

JUAN. *(Por el teléfono que suena.)* ¡Bah! ¡Majaderías! *(A Carmela:)* No contestes. Ya se cansarán de llamar. *(Suena otra vez el teléfono.)*

CARMELA. *(Contestando el teléfono.)* Casualmente aquí está. *(A Juan:)* Te llama el secretario de la Cámara . . .

JUAN. No estoy.

CARMELA. *(Al teléfono:)* Tenga la bondad de decirme de lo que se trata . . . ¿Eh? *(A Juan:)* Que tiene para ti un mensaje de don Ramón Torres . . .

JUAN. ¡Don Ramón! *(Al teléfono, forzando la voz a veces, porque llegan otra vez aplausos, silbidos y gritos:)* ¿Aló? . . . Sí . . . Que don Ramón quiere tener conmigo un . . . ¿qué? . . . ¡Ah! Un tête-à-tête. ¿Dónde dice? ¿En la oficina de usted? . . . ¿Y qué tengo yo que hablar con ese individuo? Entiendo. En esa forma menos mal. Sí . . . ¿Cuándo? Ahora no . . . no . . . Que ahora no puedo hablar con él . . . Dentro de quince minutos. Y si no que lo deje . . . *(Al colgar le hace un gesto de incomprensión a Carmela, y medita un instante.)* ¿Un tête-à-tête con don Ramón, yo? *(Súbitamente a Jaime:)* El que sabe de esto eres tú. Tú sabes todo lo que está pasando. Tú eres el culpable de todo . . .

CARMELA. *(Apaciguándolo.)* Cálmate, padrino . . .

COLMENERO. *(Entrando por la derecha, alicaído.)* ¿Se puede?

JUAN. ¡Válgame Dios! Y usted, ¿por qué no está en la sala para reseñar el debate a su antojo como de costumbre?

COLMENERO. Porque a pesar de lo que opinan mis amigos yo soy una persona decente. He venido a decírselo a don Buenaventura . . .

JUAN. ¡Hombre, no le vaya a dar una noticia así de repente!

COLMENERO. Quiero que él sepa que yo no fui quien escribió lo que va a salir en la edición de *La Voz* que está a punto de entrar en prensa. Yo ya no trabajo en *La Voz*. Se me podrá acusar de darles color a mis informaciones, pero a mí nadie me obliga a escribir lo que me consta que no es cierto . . .

JAIME. ¿A qué se refiere usted? ¿A los cien mil?

COLMENERO. Don Ramón mandó a escribir cincuenta mil nada más . . .

JAIME. ¿Y si yo le enseñara a usted . . . ? *(Llegan más gritos y silbidos que nunca, por lo que Jaime hace una pausa.)* ¿Y si yo le enseñara a usted . . . una elocuentísima carta?

COLMENERO. ¿Qué? ¿Ahora que yo me he quedado en la calle? ¿Caí de inocente? ¿Yo? ¿Un repórter estrella?

JUAN. *(A Carmela:)* Por favor, ¿tú oyes lo que yo, o estoy soñando? Dime, que la cabeza me está dando vueltas . . .

CARMELA. Los dos estamos soñando. *(Entra Buenaventura por la derecha, excitado, con el mallete todavía en la mano.)*

BUENAVENTURA. *(Sin poder ocultar su derrota.)* ¡Qué victoria! ¡Juan, qué victoria! *(A Carmela:)* Búscame a Peñita, que está por los corredores . . . *(Sale Carmela por la derecha.)* ¡Qué victoria!

JUAN. Lo dices con una cara que . . . ¡Vamos! ¡Qué victoria . . . para ellos! ¿No?

BUENAVENTURA. ¡Mía, Juan!

JUAN. ¡Ah, triunfaste!

BUENAVENTURA. Mía . . . Mía . . . *(Sube hasta el escritorio para colocar el mallete.)*

JUAN. Me lo esperaba. A ti no hay quien te derrote. En el momento decisivo de la votación . . . Al contarse los votos . . .

BUENAVENTURA. *(Arriba, en el estrado, volviéndose.)* ¡Mi voto! El mío únicamente contra todos los demás. ¡Pero, Juan, me han aplaudido dos burgueses honrados que había en las galerías!

COLMENERO. Lo que yo quiero saber es una cosa . . .

JAIME. *(Interrumpiéndolo.)* Vamos, yo le contaré.

BUENAVENTURA. *(Recogiendo y entregándole el mallete a Jaime.)* Toma, de una vez dámele al vicepresidente . . .

JUAN. *(A Jaime y Colmenero:)* ¡Un momento! Ustedes no se van todavía . . . *(A Buenaventura:)* Estos dos se traen una madeja de cosas . . . Los necesitas aquí . . .

BUENAVENTURA. ¿Que yo los necesito? ¡Vamos, hombre! Déjalos

ir. Mi cerebro es un faro de luz que navega siempre a puerto seguro: lo mismo por las mordeduras de las rocas que por la grama enflorecida… *(Jaime, disgustado, hace señal a Colmenero de que lo acompañe, y ambos salen por la derecha. Pausa. Con patética sinceridad.)* Juan, estamos en campaña. ¡Por los derechos del pueblo! ¡Por la felicidad de los oprimidos! *(Empieza a bajar del estrado.)*

JUAN. Hoy te noto distinto… algo raro…

BUENAVENTURA. ¡Oh, no! Nada. Igual que siempre. A no ser el ansia de empezar la pelea. Búscate la lista de todos nuestros líderes…

JUAN. La que teníamos aquí se ha extraviado.

BUENAVENTURA. No importa. Tráela así. O mejor déjalo. Usaremos la que está en la oficina del partido. Tenemos que convocar una asamblea del partido en seguida. Me siento como César cuando iba a cortarle la lengua al Mudo Gordiano.

JUAN. ¿Una asamblea del partido en estos momentos? Es peligroso. Hay muchos líderes disgustados que no se atreven hacerte frente, pero si les das una oportunidad… Si llegan a organizarse…

BUENAVENTURA. Tú que lo conoces bien, ¿cómo está Demetrio, el de la Unión de Sastres?

JUAN. Desde que tú le desechaste aquel proyecto ordenando a todos los empleados del Gobierno usar uniformes… fabricados por él…

BUENAVENTURA. ¿Y Matías, el de los Oficios de Construcción?

JUAN. ¿Te has olvidado de que él fue quien pasó la cuenta por la reparación del puente sobre el río Guanabara?

BUENAVENTURA. Y después yo averigüé que el tal río Guanabara no existía… ¿Y Castro, el de Sabana Seca?

JUAN. Tú le diste una beca al hijo; y una subasta, siendo el postor más alto, a su cuñado; y cuatro colocaciones a sus cuatro hermanas; y una pensión sin motivo a su madre política; y un viaje, a costa del partido, a su tío; y un solar del gobierno a su sobrino; pero corno al novio de la prima segunda de su mujer solamente le duplicaste el sueldo . . .

BUENAVENTURA. ¡Ah, sí! Él quería que se lo triplicara. Sobrinos, primos, hermanas, la suegra, la familia entera en el gobierno . . . ¡Nicotismo!

JUAN. La verdad, Ventura, es que nos hemos echado muchos enemigos . . . Eres demasiado estricto. Un jefe de partido tiene que . . . Pero, Ventura, a ti te ocurre algo . . . Se te nota en la cara . . .

BUENAVENTURA. ¡Nada, nada, Juan! Yo te aseguro que aplasto esa plaga de ingratos. Esa catacumba de desleales no podrá detenerme a mí. ¡No! Yo te aseguro que para detenerme a mí no hay más que un medio: una bala en el peritórneo . . . Corno detuvieron a aquella santa . . . *(Señala el retrato de su mujer en la pared.)* Pero mientras yo viva en el mundo de los vivos . . . Mientras yo tenga mi inteligencia y mis fuerzas . . . Tócame. Estoy fuerte. Estoy fuerte, ¿verdad? ¿No me sientes fuerte? Toca esos músculos que me dieron los muelles. A mí no me derrota nadie. Nadie . . . Yo soy invencible . . .

JUAN. Ventura, a estas horas yo no sé cuál es la situación exacta, pero si tú tienes que caer . . . no te quedes con todo el sitio . . . Déjame un par de metros a tu lado.

BUENAVENTURA. *(Abrazándolo con emoción.)* ¡Juan!

JUAN. *(Notando que Buenaventura ha sufrido en sus brazos un ligero síncope.)* ¿Qué es esto? ¿Qué te sucede? ¡Ventura! *(Lo lleva a una silla y le echa aire.)* ¡Ventura! ¡Ventura!

BUENAVENTURA. *(Aspirando profundamente.)* ¡Ah! ¡Hidrógeno!

JUAN. Nunca tomas las medicinas . . .

BUENAVENTURA. Inútil tratar de ocultártelo, Juan, mi más fiel amigo . . . Esto va más hondo . . . más hondo . . . Los años cuentan . . . o tal vez sean los achaques . . . o el cansancio . . . Quizás las decepciones . . . Pero por primera vez en mi vida . . . por primera vez . . . estoy sintiendo terror a la derrota . . . a la derrota definitiva.

JUAN. *(Dándole ánimo.)* ¿Por una pequeña escaramuza en la Cámara? ¡Bah! ¿Quién te va a derrotar a ti?

BUENAVENTURA. No sé . . . *(Tocándose el corazón.)* Siento algo aquí adentro . . . *(Espantado de su propia confesión.)* ¡Que no lo sepa nadie, Juan! ¡Que no lo sepan, porque me devoran!

JUAN. ¡No faltaba más! ¿Por quién me tomas?

BUENAVENTURA. *(Todavía se da unos golpes sobre el corazón.)* Pero si tú me ayudas, Juan; si tú me animas . . . Prométeme que tú . . .

JUAN. Cálmate, Ventura, has perdido la serenidad . . . No eres el mismo . . .

BUENAVENTURA. *(Se levanta. Medita un instante. Con una súbita esperanza remota.)* Juan, dime, ¿tú no crees que Domínguez caería de nuestra parte? Lo salvé de ir a la cárcel . . .

JUAN. Se queja de que tú no lo repusiste en su cargo.

BUENAVENTURA. ¿Después de haberse desfalcado?

JUAN. Como él dice que fue solamente por dos mil pesos . . .

BUENAVENTURA. *(Seguro de otra decepción.)* ¿Y . . . y Ambrosio?

JUAN. ¿El carbonero? Tu peor enemigo.

BUENAVENTURA. *(Sin sorpresa siquiera.)* La semana pasada lo hice Encargado de los Monumentos Históricos . . .

JUAN. Precisamente: Encargado. Pero su mujer quería que se llamara presidente. No lo hiciste presidente de los monumentos. Desengáñate.

BUENAVENTURA. *(Sentándose.)* Cualquiera creería que nos hemos quedado insólitos . . . *(Viendo a Peñita, que entra por la derecha.)* ¡Ah, tú, Peñita! *(A Juan, despreciativo:)* He aquí nuestra obra.

PEÑITA. Me dijo Carmela que usted quería hablarme.

BUENAVENTURA. ¿Qué les hiciste a mis diputados para que me silbaran?

JUAN. El culpable fue Jaime.

BUENAVENTURA. ¿Jaime? ¡Bah! Éste: el electricista sin empleo que yo transformé en secretario de obras públicas. ¿No fuiste tú mismo quien hizo construir todo esto *(Por el estrado.)* porque, según decías, yo debía estar como en un trono?

PEÑITA. Le voy a poner las cartas sobre la mesa. Jaime consiguió una parte de los diputados, los más radicales, con lo que anda diciendo de usted . . . La otra parte, la de la derecha, la consiguió un servidor.

BUENAVENTURA. ¡Tú conseguir a nadie!

PEÑITA. Con la ayuda de don Ramón . . .

BUENAVENTURA. ¡Ah! *(Levantándose.)* Bonita mezcla para combatir a un hombre: oro y baba. *(Entran por la derecha el Director y el Administrador.)* Pero oye bien esto, Peñita . . .

PEÑITA. Peña . . .

BUENAVENTURA. *(Más alto.)* Oye bien esto, Peñita . . .

PEÑITA. Peña . . .

BUENAVENTURA. *(Imponiéndose.)* Oye bien esto, Peñita: yo soy invencible; a mí no me derrota nada, ni nadie, ni nada y nadie juntos . . . Yo estoy acostumbrado a dominar los antros en donde convergen todos los vientos huracanados más terribles: *(Señalando un punto cardinal para cada uno.)* el céfiro, el austro, el ábrego, el cierzo . . . *(La excitación le ha producido otro pequeño síncope, pero Juan ha acudido a tiempo. Temblándole las rodillas, logra subir los peldaños del estrado, ayudado de Juan, y se sienta en su escritorio. A Peñita, recogiendo energía para un reto:)* ¿Lo oyes? A mí no hay quien me . . . *(Reflejando con horror el terrible pensamiento que ha cruzado por su mente.)* ¡No! Las fieras no podrán devorarme . . .

PEÑITA. Esta maldita presidencia se le ha ido a usted a la cabeza hasta el punto de no querer atender los consejos de sus amigos. ¿Qué es lo que buscamos nosotros? Mantener el partido en el poder rodeándolo de las asistencias económicas necesarias. Eso de ideales está muy bien en la oposición, cuando no hay más remedio que tenerlos, porque no se puede tener otra cosa. Pero ahora somos un partido de gobierno. ¿Qué es lo que usted pretende, que los diputados sufran los más cruentos sacrificios por conquistar sus escaños para luego regresar a sus casas como si no hubieran jamás puesto el pie en la Tierra Prometida? ¡Valiente estímulo para la lucha obrera! ¡No chantaje! ¡No soborno! ¡Viva el hambre! Pero, por Dios, ¿es ese el mejoramiento social que usted predica; el espíritu del ahorro, tan necesario? ¿Y los hijos? ¡Que se fastidien los hijos! ¿Es ese el ejemplo que debe dar un padre honrado? ¡Qué horror! Usted es un destructor de hogares. ¡El hogar, la base de la patria! Usted es un traidor al bienestar de la patria.

DIRECTOR. Si no estoy confundiendo una sonata con una mazurca . . . *(Satisfecho de la frase espera inútilmente la admiración de los oyentes.)* Si no estoy confundiendo una . . . eh . . . eh . . . ¿Usted quiere decir que hay dinero corriendo por alguna parte . . . , señor Peña?

PEÑITA. Don Ramón Torres se ha retirado de la dirección de sus negocios, pero quiere dejar su misión completa. Él cree—con sobrada razón—que su capital jamás estará seguro con este hombre en el poder. Y ha levantado un fondo para aplastarlo. Cincuenta mil . . . cien mil . . . medio millón . . . Lo que sea necesario para impedir que el país sea destruido por los caprichos legislativos de un loco . . .

BUENAVENTURA. *(Levantándose, con indignación.)* ¡Caprichos legislativos mi obra social! Peñita . . . *(Adelantándose a la interrupción de Peñita.)* Cállate, que quiero oír hablar a un hombre de talento. *(Peñita busca al hombre de talento a su alrededor.)* Peñita, repito, te di un cargo, pero no pude darte una conciencia, que te hacía más falta. Tú no sabes con quien se han metido. *(Da unos pasos trastabillando en el estrado y se coloca frente a su escritorio, en el cual se apoya.)*

PEÑITA. ¡Bah, usted está caído! El partido tendrá otro presidente dentro de cuarenta y ocho horas. Cualquiera . . . menos usted.

BUENAVENTURA. No, no es conmigo. Es con el pueblo . . . con las grandes masas del pueblo . . . con los infelices, con los hambrientos, con los oprimidos, con los miserables . . . con los huérfanos . . . con los enfermos sin salud . . . con las viudas cuyos esposos han muerto . . . Mis leyes sociales tienen que ser aprobadas. Serán aprobadas. Yo te aseguro que serán aprobadas por la mayor unanimidad imaginable de todos los presentes . . .

CARMELA. *(Entrando por el foro.)* Papá . . . tu legislación social . . . en la Cámara . . .

BUENAVENTURA. *(Ufano.)* Oyelo, Peñita . . .

CARMELA. Acaba de ser derrotada toda. Sin debate . . . sin ruido . . . en bloque . . . unánimemente . . . Derrotada toda . . .

BUENAVENTURA. *(Reprochándolo, en un grito ahogado.)* ¡Peñita, Peñita!

PEÑITA. Don José Miguel Peña y Redondo, secretario de obras públicas. ¡Más respeto! *(Sale por la derecha.)*

JUAN. *(Sacudiendo a Buenaventura, que sigue sumido en la catástrofe.)*

¡Ventura! ¡Ventura! ¿Y ahora, Ventura? Todo está perdido. ¡Es inútil luchar! Nos hemos quedado solos.

BUENAVENTURA. *(Tras un momento de meditación se rehace gradualmente.)* ¡Oh, no! Deja que yo mueva la opinión del partido . . .

JUAN. El partido se nos ha ido de las manos.

BUENAVENTURA. No importa. ¡Deja que yo mueva la opinión del pueblo! Ya los verás achacarse la responsabilidad los unos a los otros entonando el mea culpa. Ya los verás proponer levantarle un basilisco a mi memoria y celebrar el natalicio de mi esfemérides. Deja que yo agite las muchedumbres desesperadas. Los verás aprobar mis proyectos. Si me los derrotan hoy, me los pasarán mañana; si me los derrotan mañana. me los pasarán hoy. Carmela, búscame a Jaime, *(Como si se tratara de un muchacho que ha hecho una travesura.)* que voy a darle un tirón de orejas. *(Sale Carmela por la derecha.)* Y tú, Juan, avísale a . . . a . . . *(No halla a quien avisar.)* ¿Se podrá avisarle siquiera a Concha?

DIRECTOR. *(Disgustado.)* Concha salió desde esta mañana . . . con su hijita Concepción . . .

ADMINISTRADOR. *(Ídem.)* A pasarse unos días en Villa Fortuna. ¡Habráse visto! . . .

JUAN. ¿Villa Fortuna? ¿La de don Ramón?

DIRECTOR. *(Asintiendo.)* Esto sí que tiene . . . bemoles. ¿Eh?

JUAN. *(Temiendo haber perdido su cita.)* Pero don Ramón no se ha ido también, ¿no? No, no puede haberse ido. Ustedes me dispensan un momento. Se me estaba pasando la hora. *(Recuperando la seguridad.)* Tengo un tête-à-tête . . . *(Olímpicamente despreciativo.)* ¡con un canalla! *(Se dirige a la puerta de la derecha con firme determinación.)*

BUENAVENTURA. ¡Nada de violencias, Juan! Acuérdate de mi lema: nada de violencias si no hay que pegarle a alguien. ¡Te lo prohíbo! *(Sale Juan por la derecha sin prestar oído.)*

DIRECTOR. *(Al Administrador:)* Vamos.

BUENAVENTURA. ¡Oh, no se vayan tan pronto! No saben ustedes cómo les agradezco que estén conmigo en esta lucha contra don Ramón.

DIRECTOR. *(Tratando de zafarse.)* Sí, sí, don Ramón . . . Pero nosotros creíamos . . . Estas nuevas circunstancias que se han presentado . . . A la verdad, hoy andamos de prisa . . .

BUENAVENTURA. ¡Si ni siquiera me han dicho a qué han venido! Veamos. *(Se sienta en un escalón del estrado y los invita a que se le unan, lo cual los otros evidentemente consideran contrario a su dignidad.)* Siéntense . . . Siéntense . . .

ADMINISTRADOR. Se trataba meramente de un proyecto de ley que se le ocurrió a éste *(El Director.)* para la educación de los pobres . . .

DIRECTOR. De las pobres, de las pobrecitas . . . Educación musical . . . Es una vergüenza que voces tan ricas como las que pueden hallarse en muchas obreritas encantadoras se pierdan sin llegar a la ópera . . .

CARMELA. *(Entrando por la derecha, seguida de Jaime.)* Aquí está Jaime.

ADMINISTRADOR. Si a éste, como director del conservatorio, y a mí, como diletante, se nos constituyese por ley en una Junta de Becas, con facultad para seleccionar dos docenas de muchachitas de voz fresca . . .

DIRECTOR. Una docena cada uno . . . *(Dándose un beso en los dedos.)* ¡Oh! *(Buenaventura ni siquiera se molesta en gastar palabras en ellos. Con un cansado ademán les indica que se vayan.)*

ADMINISTRADOR. ¿Eh?

DIRECTOR. ¡Cómo! ¿Nos bota? *(Buenaventura vuelve a indicarles que le hagan el favor de marcharse.)*

ADMINISTRADOR. ¡Bueno que me pase por cogerle pena! ¡Qué tenía yo que explicarle ningún proyecto si ya no lo puede hacer aprobar!

DIRECTOR. ¡Seguro! El hombre es Peñita.

ADMINISTRADOR. Sí, veamos a Peñita . . . *(Corrigiéndose, con énfasis por Buenaventura.)* ¡Al señor Peña!

JAIME. *(Que está junto a la puerta, cuando los dos pasan por su lado.)* A mí es que deben verme. Traten de ponerse al habla conmigo hoy mismo . . .

ADMINISTRADOR. ¡Ooh! *(Sale por la derecha con el Director, que por su parte se saca su malicioso silbido.)*

BUENAVENTURA. Jaime, no te reconozco. Tú has sido por años mi discípulo predilecto. Tu fe en mis ideales, tu sinceridad en mis doctrinas, me hicieron distinguirte como una futura promesa. Desde que te me presentaste, pobre muchacho huérfano salido de un auspicio, te abrí mis manos para que entraras en mi seno, y mi corazón siempre ha estado para ti herméticamente de par en par. Ni aun una misma madre que nunca haya tenido hijos, sería capaz de comprender cómo te he querido. Me has visto vencer. Me has visto construir mi humilde bohío y llevarlo por mares procelosos, siguiendo la brújula que disipa las tinieblas, hasta la clámide del éxito. *(Levantándose y yendo a él.)* Y ahora, ahora que estamos en las bicúspides del triunfo, ahora que tenemos la carga de la responsabilidad bajo nuestros hombros, ¿ahora te me vas a escapar como un soldado que ya no quiere más tremolar en alto su uniforme, para unirte a las alimañas que entretejen contra mí la baba de sus labios en el parnaso de los mentideros? Jaime, Jaime, ya no eres un niño menor de edad. Comprende. Abre los ojos y comprende. Yo tengo los brazos tendidos. Ven a ellos de nuevo.

JAIME. Ridículo, perfectamente ridículo. *(Le vuelve la espalda y se retira.)*

BUENAVENTURA. ¿Te niegas? ¿Me desprecias?

JAIME. Yo no quiero contacto con redentores que se descuelgan de la cruz por cincuenta mil pesos . . .

BUENAVENTURA. *(Con compasión.)* ¡Pobre Jaime! Me lo han vuelto loco.

JAIME. Pronto serán millares y millares y millares de locos repitiendo mis palabras. ¿Pronto? No, ya. El pueblo entero debe de estarlas repitiendo ya, gracias a una edición especial de *La Voz*. No se olvide de que yo tengo en mi poder una carta comprometedora . . .

BUENAVENTURA. *(Con pena aún.)* ¡Insensato! ¡Tú sabes los quilates del calibre de mi honradez! Tú sabes que al hombre que muere rico yo lo mandaría a fusilar. Sí, unos tiros en la región parietal *(Se señala el abdomen.)* para que aprenda a no ser egoísta. ¿Por qué has hecho esto? ¿Por qué lo has hecho?

JAIME. Porque ya yo no soy más el secretario, el pobre secretario sin brillo que no puede ni conquistar un corazón de mujer . . . Todos lograron a mi alrededor lo que querían: dinero, posición social, aplausos . . . Yo, nada. Yo . . . corregir disparates ajenos en las declaraciones para la prensa. Basta ya.

BUENAVENTURA. Precisamente siempre has llamado la atención por lo inadvertido que pasas. Pero tú tenías un gran destino, que podía leerlo en las estrellas cualquier urólogo. Tú al fin hubieras acabado por sucederme en la presidencia.

JAIME. ¿Al fin? Desde ahora. *(Subiendo al estrado.)* Ahora voy a ser yo el presidente del partido. Si hay que decir disparates, yo soy quien voy a decirlos.

BUENAVENTURA. ¿Tú? ¿Sin la experiencia del discurso de los tiempos? ¿Sin el desarrollo progresivo que lleva al conjunto total?

JAIME. Sí, yo. Innumerables líderes me han prometido ya sus votos. ¡Yo!

BUENAVENTURA. Ahora descubro las negras tinieblas en que vio la luz esa idea. No es tuya. Te la infiltraron los que te vinieron con turbios oropeles de arboladura verbilocua . . . Gente comprada por don Ramón para tentarte como a Satanás . . .

JAIME. Don Ramón o no, yo seré el jefe . . . el que mande.

BUENAVENTURA. No, Jaime, aun cuando fueras asaltado a la presidencia, que no serás asaltado, no mandarías tú. Mandaría don Ramón . . .

JAIME. ¡Don Ramón! Tan pronto tenga yo la presidencia ya verá usted a las masas trabajadoras quemarle las fábricas a don Ramón, saquearle la casa, repartir sus tierras, perseguirlo por las calles como a un perro . . .

BUENAVENTURA. Peor. Entonces tampoco serias tú el que mandarías. Mandaría ese rencor que te consume; mandaría la mezquindad de que has comenzado a ser esclavo. Mi doctrina la has delegado al olvido: amor, amor; por amor al desvalido combatir contra el poderoso, por amor a la justicia combatir el atropello . . . Incendios, sabotajes, huelgas, protestas, por amor, no por odio . . . ¡Por amor!

JAIME. ¡Amor! *(Ríe con una seca risa nerviosa.)* ¡Amor! ¡Qué sabe usted de amor! *(A Carmela, llegando junto a ella:)* Tú, qué sabes tú de amor . . . ¡Amor! ¡No me venga con cuentos de hadas!

BUENAVENTURA. *(Viendo entrar a Tirado, que viene cargando con la maquinilla robada en el Club.)* ¿Por qué dejan pasar este hombre? ¿Ya se acabó la privacidad aquí?

CARMELA. No hay nadie en la antesala. Yo he sido quien la ha estado atendiendo.

TIRADO. Usted dispense . . . Yo me retiro . . .

JAIME. No, puede quedarse. Yo soy quien me voy. ¿Sabe a dónde, don Buena? A la manifestación de protesta contra usted.

BUENAVENTURA. ¿Manifestación?

JAIME. No debe tardar. Pasará por aquí al frente. Nuestros líderes la están formando. Les hablaré yo . . . ¡Yo! Para ponerles sobre aviso . . . para leer esta carta . . . para contarles cómo puede un hombre vender a su hija . . . Les hablaré yo, el nuevo presidente. *(Sale por la derecha.)*

CARMELA. ¡Y yo creía que era amor lo que me profesaba! ¡Amor! Un alma tan pequeña no puede sentir amor. ¡Era grosería reprimida que ahora estalla! ¿No te parece, papá?

BUENAVENTURA. *(Sale de su abstracción, la mira con ternura, le hace una caricia. En el momento en que va a contestar reconoce el objeto que tiene Tirado en las manos.)* ¡Ah, mi máquina! ¡Falta que me iba a hacer para esta campaña! ¡Qué artículos me van a salir ahora! *(La coge y la lleva a su escritorio.)*

TIRADO. *(Acercándose al estrado.)* Señor presidente . . . Usted ve . . . Yo he sido leal con usted . . . Hasta le he traído esta maquinilla que usted quería recuperar, quitándosela a un primo mío que la tenía. Pero si usted me lo permite . . . Yo quisiera hacerle una pregunta.

BUENAVENTURA. Sí, hombre, pregunta.

TIRADO. *(Cohibido.)* Por ahí andan diciendo que usted está caído . . . Y yo me he negado a creerlo. "No creas nada, Tirado—me he dicho—, hasta que él mismo no te lo confiese. Tú hasta el último momento debes serle leal."

BUENAVENTURA. ¡Ah, Tirado! *(Bajando y echándole el brazo por el hombro.)* Nunca imaginé que me fueras tan edicto. ¿Qué más se te da mi suerte?

TIRADO. Bueno . . . es que si es cierto que usted está caído . . .

(Retirándose un poco.) yo me llevo la máquina otra vez . . . *(Entra Juan por la derecha, vacilante y nervioso.)*

BUENAVENTURA. ¡Ah, Juan! *(Susto de éste.)* Al fin llegas. Ya el camino está claro. Ahora, a pelear. A dar nuestra batalla definitiva. Yo no cedo un ábside.

JUAN. *(Inseguro.)* Sí . . . , sí . . .

BUENAVENTURA. A fertilizar el ambiente para estructurar el camino que nos empuje a la victoria . . . Apunta eso, Juan, que estoy de vena . . . *(Juan saca su libreta y abandona la escritura apenas la comienza.)* Las trincheras que levante hasta el cielo la impotencia de los que me ataquen, yo se las derribaré con un solo martillazo del crisol incólume de mi vida, que está grabada en los anaqueles de la protohistoria . . . Apunta, Juan, apunta . . . *(Juan no apunta.)* Yo voy a decirle al pueblo la verdad tangente. Yo les hablaré los lunes, miércoles y viernes . . . y etcéteramente los demás días de la semana. Yo . . .

JUAN. Ventura . . . *(La libreta y el lápiz que tenía en las manos las tira al canasto.)* Ventura . . . es infantil engañarnos . . . No nos rompamos la cabeza contra la pared . . . Estamos solos . . .

BUENAVENTURA. Más lo estábamos hace veinte años.

JUAN. Éramos jóvenes entonces . . . Tú no sufrías síncopes . . .

BUENAVENTURA. Con tu fuerza basta para los dos, si tú me ayudas . . .

JUAN. Es que ya yo tampoco soy el de antes. ¿No me lo has notado últimamente?

BUENAVENTURA. No. Yo te veo como siempre. A menos que yo esté necesitando espejuelos de esos bisexuales . . .

JUAN. He venido callando mis achaques por no alarmarte . . .

BUENAVENTURA. ¡Ah, pobre Juan! ¿Y crees que voy a permitir que ahora que estás enfermo cometan contigo un ostracismo?

¿Que te manden a morir a un hospital cualquiera? No, esta pelea la doy yo solo. Y la gano, Juan. Y la gano. Dime, ¿qué te sientes?

JUAN. El pulso . . . ¿sabes? El corazón . . . Fíjate en mis ojeras . . .

BUENAVENTURA. ¿Qué?

JUAN. Un grupo de media docena de amigos me ha recomendado mucho un viaje a Alemania . . . a ver al doctor Schmidt . . .

BUENAVENTURA. ¡Juan!

JUAN. ¿Qué te ocurre?

BUENAVENTURA. Nada . . . Nada . . . *(Sin poder ocultar su dolor, sube, trastabillando, hasta su escritorio.)* Dime: ¿vas a ver también al doctor Foncé, en París?

JUAN. ¿Ah, lo conoces? Sí. Es el primero que veré. Parto mañana mismo. *(Buenaventura se desliza hasta caer en la silla, con el rostro contra el escritorio.)* ¡Ventura! *(Corriendo a él.)* ¡Ventura! ¿Qué te sucede? ¡Tú estás enfermo! Te lo decía. Estás muy enfermo.

CARMELA. *(Acudiendo.)* ¡Papá! ¡Papá!

BUENAVENTURA. Está bien. Ya pasó. Hoy estamos aquí; mañana quizás dónde. ¡Qué más da! *(A Tirado:)* ¡Eh, tú! . . . *(Por la máquina.)* Llévatela. *(Tirado sale con la máquina muy agradecido.)* Juan, se te hace tarde para tus preparativos de viaje . . .

JUAN. Es cierto. Voy. No te olvides de tus medicinas. *(En la puerta de la derecha, confuso, tropieza con Colmenero que entra con una cámara fotográfica y un periódico en las manos.)* Dispense. ¡Ah, una noticia para su periódico! Mañana . . . *(Dolorosamente turbado.)* mañana . . . hoy . . . Ventura que le diga de mi viaje. *(Sale por la derecha. Buenaventura ahoga un sollozo y se doblega de nuevo sobre el escritorio.)*

COLMENERO. Don Ventura, a mí me han aceptado de nuevo en *La Voz* con la condición de que obtenga de usted unas declaraciones sobre la noticia . . . *(Leyendo los titulares.)* PRESIDENTE DE LA CÁMARA SOBORNADO. VENDIÓ LEGISLACIÓN SOCIAL POR CINCUENTA MIL PESOS. ¿Qué tiene usted que decir? Piense que si no llevo esta información vuelven a despedirme. ¡Don Ventura, por favor! Deme la exclusiva.

BUENAVENTURA. *(Levantando la cabeza.)* ¿Ah?

COLMENERO. Esto de los cincuenta mil . . . ¿Es cierto?

BUENAVENTURA. *(Casi inconsciente, quizás con un vago deseo de acabarlo todo de una vez.)* Es cierto.

CARMELA. ¡Papá! ¡Papá! ¡No!

COLMENERO. Una fotografía ahora reflejando sus sentimientos al leer *La Voz* . . . De pie . . . De cuerpo entero . . . Tenga el periódico . . . *(Buenaventura se deja alzar sin voluntad. Se oyen algunos gritos lejanos; confusos compases de marcha.)*

BUENAVENTURA. *(A Carmela, cobrando vida gradualmente:)* ¡Óyelos! ¿Los oyes? ¡Óyelos! *(Apoyándose en Carmela, baja como un autómata hacia la ventana, para desesperación de Colmenero, a quien se le retrasa su fotografía.)* ¡Óyelos, Carmela! *(Ya en la ventana.)* ¡Ah, allá vienen!

CARMELA. Cálmate, cálmate, papá . . .

BUENAVENTURA. Óyelos. *(Se oye la gritería y la música de la manifestación que se acerca.)* Ahí vienen los buenos . . . los honrados . . . *(Colmenero rápidamente le prende al pecho un cartón con un número, mientras Carmela mira por la ventana.)* Pasan los redentores del pueblo . . .

COLMENERO. *(Enfoca y lo llama.)* ¡Ahora! ¡Don Buena! *(Buenaventura y Carmela vuelven el rostro. Brilla el relámpago de la instantánea.)* ¡Ah! ¡Padre e hija! ¡Con el número en el pecho para dar una idea de como se vería en el presidio! ¡Qué sensación va a causar esto! *(Sale corriendo por la derecha.)*

CARMELA. ¡Papá! ¡Papá! *(Le arranca y rompe indignada el número.)*

BUENAVENTURA. *(Como un sonámbulo.)* ¡Óyelos! ¡Óyelos! *(Se escuchan los gritos y silbidos de la gente contra Buenaventura.)* Mira a Jaime, al frente. Mira a Peñita. ¡Juntos! *(Como si quisiera gritarlo por la ventana, pero en realidad con desfallecimiento.)* ¡Vivan! ¡Vivan ambos! ¡Los buenos, los honrados!

CARMELA. Ven, ven, descansa. *(Rompiendo los cristales de la ventana caen piedras que tiran de la calle.)* Nos apedrean, ven. *(Consigue retirarlo de la ventana.)*

BUENAVENTURA. ¡Años y años luchando! ¡Mi vida entera! ¡Mi vida entera creyendo que bastaba construir sobre el dolor del pueblo para construir sobre roca! Y ahora siento que el mundo tiembla bajo mis pies . . . ¿No lo sientes, Carmela, no lo sientes cómo se estremece? *(Carmela lo hace sentar en una silla.)*

JORGE. *(Entrando rebosante de felicidad por la derecha.)* ¡Carmelita! ¡Carmelita! Acabamos de acordar cumplir por nuestra cuenta en todas nuestras empresas los fines que perseguía la legislación social *(Volviéndose a Buenaventura.)* suya . . . Haremos un fondo, un gran fondo; y nuestros trabajadores tendrán todas las ventajas que usted propulsa.

DON RAMÓN. *(Entrando precipitadamente por la derecha.)* ¡Qué locura es esa, Jorge? Ya me enteraron por teléfono. Apenas te entrego la dirección de nuestros negocios, quieres destruirlo todo . . .

JORGE. ¿Te vas a oponer?

DON RAMÓN. ¿Pero es que tú crees justo que nuestras empresas compitan en desventaja? No, nosotros solos no. Con estos gastos va a cargar todo el que tenga dos perras . . .

JORGE. ¿Qué te propones?

DON RAMÓN. Hacer aprobar toda esa legislación social hoy mismo, revisada por mí para que ningún competidor la evada. Ya pagará el pueblo en definitiva . . .

BUENAVENTURA. *(Levantándose trabajosamente señala el retrato en la pared.)* ¿Ese retrato es mío . . . o es otro mueble más?

CARMELA. *(Extrañada.)* Propiedad pública, papá.

BUENAVENTURA. ¡Y era lo único que hubiera querido llevarme!

CARMELA. *(Cada vez más extrañada.)* ¿A casa?

BUENAVENTURA. A los muelles . . . Vuelvo a mi gente . . .

DON RAMÓN. ¿No está usted contento con la realización de su programa social? Ya verá usted los elogios que le va a tributar *La Voz* . . .

BUENAVENTURA. *(Regresando espiritualmente de muy lejos.)* ¿Mi programa? ¿Dijo usted mi programa? Mi programa . . . *(Súbitamente se yergue, lleno de un nuevo valor, como en sus buenos tiempos.)* No, ése no es mi pustulado de apóstol . . . *(Subiendo muy agitado a su escritorio, de cuyas gavetas saca los papeles para llevárselos.)* No, eso no es por lo que yo he luchado toda mi vida . . . No vale la pena luchar por tan poco . . .

DON RAMÓN. ¿Por qué, entonces?

CARMELA. ¿Por qué, papá?

BUENAVENTURA. Por primera vez veo claro el camino. Por primera vez una luz me ilumina. Es un rayo de luz que viene de la altura. Me siento nuevo. Me siento joven. *(Como contestando una voz que parece haber oído.)* Sí, sí, voy a emprender de nuevo la lucha.

DON RAMÓN. Díganos sus nuevas ideas para ver si podemos complacerlo.

BUENAVENTURA. Estas ideas hay que bautizarlas primero con sangre de infelices para que puedan entenderse . . . Y el bautismo espera . . . ¿No oyen ustedes esa voz? ¿No la oyen? ¿No la oyen cómo me pregunta por los pulmones desgarrados de los obreros, por los huérfanos sin pan? ¿No la oyen cómo grita desde los asilos, desde las cárceles, desde las tumbas? ¿No oyen su estrépito? ¿Su espantoso estrépito? No la oyen que grita que todo esto se cae, que se desploma. ¡Se desploma y nos aplasta!

JORGE. Yo estoy dispuesto a hacer cualquier reforma . . . Cualquiera.

BUENAVENTURA. *(Sin atenderlo.)* Me esperan . . . Lejos de todo esto . . . Mi talento inmortal . . . Mi obra . . . Me esperan . . .

CARMELA. ¡Estás delirando, papá!

BUENAVENTURA. *(Incoherentemente.)* En la democracia . . . en la libertad . . . en el dolor . . . ¡No! . . . Estoy fuerte . . . No podrán devorarme . . .

CARMELA. *(Viendo que Buenaventura está a punto de derrumbarse.)* ¡Papá! ¡Papá!

BUENAVENTURA. En el amor . . . en el amor . . . *(Cae y rueda por los peldaños.)*

TELON

TEATRO DE LA UNIVERSIDAD

Septiembre 23, 1940.

Estreno de la comedia dramática en Tres Actos
de Luis Rechani Agrait

MI SEÑORÍA

VALOR: $1.00

Ticket for the premiere of *Mi señoría* at the theater of the University of Puerto Rico, Río Piedras. Courtesy of Jonathan Cohen.

AFTERWORD

Luis Rechani Agrait and Modern Puerto Rican Drama

Luis Rechani Agrait (1902–1994) was part of the Generation of the 1930s in Puerto Rico, the group that established modern theater on the island. Beginning in 1938 with the drama competition sponsored by the Ateneo Puertorriqueño (Puerto Rican Atheneum), the diverse trends of Puerto Rican playwriting converged in a dynamic movement that generated plays on par with the best international theater. The movement's leading playwrights (and winners of the Ateneo's drama competition) were Manuel Méndez Ballester (e.g., *El clamor de los surcos*; The Cry of the Furrows), Gonzalo Arocho del Toro (e.g., *El desmonte*; The Clearing), and Fernando Sierra Berdecía (e.g., *Esta noche juega el jóker*; Tonight the Joker Plays). But Rechani came closely after with his play *Mi señoría* (*My Excellency*), which debuted in 1940 and was similarly a dramatic milestone.

A poet and journalist, Rechani initially published a book of poetry for children and a reader for second graders in the late 1920s. Before 1940, he also wrote two minor unpublished comedies: "Contra la vida" (1926; Against Life) and "Tu mujer no te engaña" (1934; Your Wife Doesn't Cheat on You). These first dramatic attempts were followed by his masterpiece *Mi señoría*. Written in 1937, the play was staged three years later by the Sociedad Dramática Areyto, a group of independent producers that was pivotal in presenting original plays by new playwrights. The growth of independent theater and the development of a theater program at the University of Puerto Rico contributed to the staging of new innovative plays. This trend culminated in 1958 when the government officially recognized this theatrical tradition with the creation of the Puerto Rican Theater Festival, an ongoing annual event that presents the best of the island's plays.

There is no evidence of Rechani's new dramatic creations until 1964, when his play *Todos los ruiseñores cantan* (1964; All the Nightingales Sing) was included in the Puerto Rican Theater Festival. This inclusion was at last a recognition of Rechani's contribution to modern Puerto Rican theater. The staging was followed by *¿Cómo se llama esta flor?* (1965; What's This Flower's Name?), *Tres piraguas en un día de calor* (1970; Three Snow Cones on a Hot Day), *Llora en el atardecer la fuente* (1971; At Sunset the Fountain Weeps), *¡Oh, dorada ilusión de alas abiertas!* (1978; Oh, Golden Illusion of Open Wings!), and *El extraño caso del señor Oblomós* (1981; The Strange Case of Mr. Oblomos). Most of these plays blend poetic perspective and social context, with satire often playing a significant role.

Mi señoría is without a doubt the play that established Rechani as a major comedy writer. The plot centers on Buenaventura Padilla, an honest socialist politician who lacks refinement and general culture. The three acts are structured in a satirical sequence of his rise to power, disillusionment, and final sour decadence. The comic perspective is attained through stereotyped characters: Ramón Torres, the manipulative and heartless bourgeois; Colmenero, the journalist who sells out for the best offer; the Bugler and Tortillita, alienated cruel people. But the hilarity is located in the ignorance of the main character, Buenaventura, who pretends to be an educated politician but mixes up his language, mispronounces words, applies incorrect biblical and mythological references at random, changes grammar rules, and even proclaims himself to be—and asks to be called—My Excellency, instead of Your Excellency. For Buenaventura, Orpheus and not Morpheus is the god of sleep/dreams, the Apocalypse is the "Epoca Lisa," and the political opposition is a crowd of Abels who want to kill Cain again.

Rechani adds a subplot to the political satire with the relationship between Carmela, the daughter of Buenaventura, and Jorge (George), the son of Ramón Torres. This subplot, though trite, gives the plot a sentimental resonance that points to the playwright's intention. As love mingles with corruption, the caricatural satire blends with Buenaventura's failed honesty, creating an almost tragic character. The political leader who sincerely fights against injustice is at the same time so ridiculous in his rhetoric as to undermine his idealism. Sometimes his social proposals flow logically, then turn into a Rabelaisian hyperbole. Characterization is attained through paradox, adding new dimensions to Rechani's comedies. Farce and quixotic principles live together in his dramatic works. As Buenaventura says, "The only road to be followed, are four." Perhaps this is one of the playwright's main contributions to modern Puerto Rican theater. Thanks to Swan Isle Press, Rechani Agrait's *My Excellency,* his acclaimed masterpiece revived multiple times on the island, is now available to the English-speaking world through this magnificent translation by William Carlos Williams.

José Luis Ramos Escobar
San Juan, 2025

April 16, 1941 (1)

PORTO RICO TALK

1. A statement as to the modern basis of poetic form (informal)

2. Read some illustrative verses

3. Spanish (Portugese) and American-English. Our profitable interrelationship in developing a new poetic form : EXAMPLE - Lope de Vega vs Shakespeare as a model (form) for America : What we might profit etc etc

****

Preamble

The difficulty is to keep such a talk as this informal.

After all, there is no great point at issue. We are here for the most part to look at each other, to recognize in each other - that curious complexity called a writer, to encourage and to learn. But most to try to find a means, through the art which we practise, to communicat with each other - for what may come of it.

William Carlos Williams's typed notes for his talk at the First Inter-American Writers' Conference of the University of Puerto Rico. Courtesy of Beinecke Rare Book and Manuscript Library, Yale University.

LECTURE

An Informal Discussion of Poetic Form

The difficulty is to keep such a talk as this informal.*

After all, there is no great point at issue. We are here for the most part to look at each other, to recognize in each other that curious complexity called a writer, to encourage, and to learn. But most to try to find a means, through the art which we practice, to communicate with each other—for what may come of it.

The study of poetry is based still largely on metaphysical criteria. This makes for as many approaches to any given poem as there are schools or attitudes of thought in the world.

This richness may have its rewards, but it is likely to cause a great confusion in the mind of the student. What should be our basic attitude toward a poem, any poem, there, lying on the page? It is acceptable, repellant? Is it a work of art or a sub-mental impertinence or both?

Upon what shall a judgment be based? If we can get to that, we can get to something we can understand together.

A beginning is made toward a clarification among this swarming mixture of approaches by cutting across all categories and declaring flatly:

Every poem either is or is not related to the structural character of its own age. Then I would go on to say: that unless a poem is so related it has already lost its primary opportunity and significance.

---

*This talk was given at the First Inter-American Writers' Conference of the University of Puerto on April 16, 1941; the text with poems was published in *The University of Puerto Rico Bulletin* 12, no. 2 (December 1941): 31–44.

Drop that there and let me make another statement:

The arts are really the history of the mind. If they are cramped or inadequate, the mind will be found to have been deformed—as much so as were the feet of Chinese women, formerly, to indicate their aristocracy.

Thus we have two statements—the poem is or is not related to the structural character of its own age, *and* the poem in itself constitutes the history of the mind.

To carry the argument still further, let me insist that the poem presents the history of the mind in any age primarily by its structure—which, if the poem is to matter at all, will represent in some particular the true structure of that age which produces it.

What we need in verse today is a great technician.

We need one who can *hear* the "normal" language and who knows the patterns of the past to forget them. Then to invent, that is, to rediscover in the vernacular about him, as a fresh insight, the simple elements that, also, made up the old rigidities—and reintegrate them among the living material into adequate modern forms expansive enough to include the whole armamentarium of the mind as we know it today—forms uncramped, unclipped, uncompressed *structurally* into those past "aristocracies" which are today damnable in their deforming limitations.

The language is the thing. The language must not be deformed to fit the pattern of the verse. The verse must be transformed to fit the exigencies of the language.

By debased rigidities of pattern, if we are not careful, our vehicle of communication, our language, will be falsified, and if in its structure, you may be sure in its meaning also. We are likely to be made to say what we do not intend and to come off brutalized thereby.

Let us remember, the elements of composition are always free and available—*if* we have the genius to find them; it is only in their outworn entanglements of past usage that they tyrannize over us and need breaking down and *not* in their essence.

The cleansing and rehabilitation of the language gives the poet much of his seriousness of purpose facing the world.

So, before reading a few poems by way of illustration—let me go back a moment for emphasis, here and there, and the elaboration of one or two points:

1. There are many ways of looking at a poem, all of them misleading unless founded upon structure.

2. A poem is a use of *words* (as emphasized by Gertrude Stein) which when taken with the *structure* together comprise its form—the elements of form being: the *line* (What is it to be?) and the *word*, its selection, position, and sequence in the line.

But now something extraordinary takes place—which is the essence of poetry: the form achieved becomes itself a "word," the most significant of all, that dominates every other word in the poem.

> NOTE: Imagism, which had a use in focusing the attention upon the importance of concrete imagery in the poem, lost its place finally because as a form it completely lacked structural necessity. The image served for everything, so that the structure, a weaker and weaker free verse, degenerated finally into a condition very nearly resembling in meaninglessness that of the sonnet.
>
> The "objectivists" attempted to remedy this fault by fusing with each image a form in its own right—but there were few successes—or have been few so far.

The *structural approach* has two phases, the first, the selection of forms from poems already achieved, to restuff them with metaphysical and other matter, and, the second, to parallel the inventive impetus of other times with structural concepts derived from our own day.

The first is *weak* and the second *strong*.

> NOTE: This does not imply that the men who take the positions one way or the other are either weak or strong. The thing to remember is that weak and strong are *both* phases of the structural approach.

The weak approach (to the intricacies of poetic form) is typified by the teaching attitude. Teaching—that is, the academy—is predominantly weak in this respect. It can't be otherwise, and this, in fact, is its strength. It is the throne of precedent. But because of this it tends to arrogate to itself, mistakenly, prerogatives which, sometimes, it does not serve.

The *strong* approach—made through the vernacular by attention in its modulated character, inventing from that—is relegated too often to the services of outlaws. Over long periods the weak approach tends to culminate in the strong, establishing the peaks of literature.

> NOTE: The validity of this entire proposal (that structure is of such preeminent importance in a poem) has been questioned by the academy, the point being raised that Villon did not invent but took over the ballad, a form hackneyed by court use, in his day almost a popular game. But Villon dignified it to such powerful advantage that his use of it constitutes in itself a unique meaning, an excellent example of just that strong approach through the vernacular which I wish to show.

New concepts will always call for new forms, and new forms demand new structures. The basis of new poetic forms will always be the language of that age which demands of them its fullest expression.

In hearing the following poems, please remember that modern poetry is not selective—as poetry in the past has been. It is inclusive and comprehensive by its definition: to raise or enlarge the imagination to new areas of understanding. It says nothing of what shall be admitted. Nothing is excluded. How can it be? Every conceivable thing is material for poetry under the structural definition.

> [Here, Williams read these poems of his: "All the Fancy Things," "Brilliant Sad Sun," "Adam," "Eve," "The

Flower," "Cancion" (his translation of verse by the Spanish Golden Age dramatist and poet Lupercio de Argensola, preceded by the original Spanish), and "To Elsie."—J.C.]

If, in a work of art, it is by the nascent form that the fullest—and most timely—significance is expressed, what function might not Latin America exercise toward the United States and Canada in this respect? To introduce us to Spanish and Portuguese literature—pure and simple. And if to that literature, to make us familiar with its forms as contrasted with our own.

For instance: *What* influence can Spanish have on us who speak a derivative of English in North America? To shake us free for a reconsideration of the poetic line.

You can suggest to us that we are not English, that the Elizabethan triumphs, except for their magnificence, concern us not at all. That is, in their formal quality they do not concern us.

Specifically, by showing us a shorter, four-stressed line rather than the pentameter; by showing us a great dramatic talent, Lope de Vega, who did not use the iambic pentameter—give that hint which will tend to free us to our own uses.

For in many ways 16th- and 17th-century Spain and Spaniards are nearer to us in the United States today than, perhaps, England ever was. It is a point worth at least taking under consideration. We in the United States are climactically as by latitude and weather much nearer Spain than England, as also in the volatility of our spirits, in racial mixture—much more like Gothic and Moorish Spain.

Even more specifically, we have a problem before us in the United States to find a verse form that will be suitable for the theater.* We

*In an interview published in *El Mundo* three days after he gave this talk, Williams said: "Creo que lo más interesante que se perfila en el campo de las letras es la vinculación del verso con el teatro, del arte lírico con el arte dramático" (I think that the most interesting thing now taking shape in the field of letters is the bond of verse with theater, of lyric art with dramatic art).

know it can never be blank verse. It may very well be that through hints from the *romancero* or at least Lope's shorter, swifter line, we will finally discover something more acceptable to our temperament, manner of thought, and speech.

We know what we should have, but we don't know how to get it. We know what we should do, but we don't know how to do it. It looks as though our salvation may come not from within ourselves but from the outside.

And if everything else that I have said is wrongheaded, destructive to that precious soul of things which the true poet should cherish! if I have been mechanical and crass in my concepts, relying for my argument on mere techniques and materials—well, in that case, from the old and alien soul of America itself, may the relics of its ancient, its pre-Columbian cultures still kindle something in me that will be elevated, profound, and common to us all, Americans. There is that path still open to us.

William Carlos Williams
Rutherford, 1941

ACKNOWLEDGMENTS

The project leading to the present book started seven years ago as part of my efforts originating in 2008 to recover the overlooked translations made by William Carlos Williams. I became a seeker, and that led to my discovery of his translation of *Mi señoría* held in the library at the University at Buffalo. This translation opened new doors for further research and exploration, including trips to Puerto Rico. It was exciting to learn about the playwright Luis Rechani Agrait and Puerto Rican theater and to discover more about Williams's path as a translator that was shaped by his deep family connection to the island, Caribbean culture, and Spanish. One step always leads to another, and now it has led to this book, *My Excellency*.

Here, I want to express my gratitude to the people and institutions that helped me complete my research and manuscript and make this book a reality: University at Buffalo Library's Poetry Collection (Alison Fraser and James Maynard); Instituto de Cultura Puertorriqueña (Institute of Puerto Rican Culture; Hilda Ayala González, Cristina Martínez Pedraza, and María Rodríguez Matos); Yale University's Beinecke Rare Book and Manuscript Library; Puerto Rican theater specialists, Myrna Casas, Lowell Fiet, and Rosa Luisa Márquez; critical readers, Daniel Deutsch, Peter Hulme, Julio Marzán, José Luis Ramos Escobar, and David Unger; Swan Isle Press team, David Rade, Elizabeth Ellingboe, Grace Ashton, and Marianne Jankowski; Daphne Williams Fox of the William Carlos Williams Estate; Ariana Philips and Jennifer Weltz of the Jean V. Naggar Literary Agency; and Miguel Garcia-Rechani and María C. Rechani, family of the playwright.

Jonathan Cohen

Luis Rechani Agrait as a boy with his father, Pío Rechani Rodrigo, and mother, María Josefa Agrait Aldea. Photograph courtesy of María C. Rechani.

BIOGRAPHIES

Luis Rechani Agrait (1902–1994) is considered one of Puerto Rico's major dramatists of the twentieth century. A journalist, poet, short-story writer, and playwright, he was known largely as a journalist when *Mi señoría* was first produced in 1940 at the University of Puerto Rico's theater. His first play to be staged, it combined both his diverse writing background and long concern with social and historical issues. He had spent several prior years living in the United States while attending first Harvard and then the University of Richmond. When he returned to Puerto Rico, he worked for the daily paper *El Mundo* as editor in chief. Public matters were the primary focus of his attention. He left the paper after a couple of years to work in the Department of Public Instruction as assistant to the commissioner. During this period he published two books for children: a reader, *Páginas de color de rosa* (Heath, 1928; Rose-Colored Pages), and a book of poems with fellow poet Rafael Rivera Otero, *Una nube en el viento* (Los autores, 1929; A Cloud in the Wind). In 1930 he returned to *El Mundo* and worked there over the next decade, during which he published several short stories, most appearing in the weekly magazine *Puerto Rico Ilustrado,* which was delivered as an insert in *El Mundo*. Stimulated by the activity in Puerto Rican theater in the late 1930s, he resumed writing drama, following his previous efforts, which had resulted in two unpublished comedies: "Contra la vida" (1926; Against Life) and "Tu mujer no te engaña" (1934; Your Wife Doesn't Cheat on You). He wrote *Mi señoría* (Puerto Rico Ilustrado, 1940; *My Excellency*) in 1937. Three years later he brought the play to the attention of a new theater company that had formed to produce experimental theater in search of a national identity, the first company on the island dedicated to a vital dramaturgy of genuine national character. Called the Sociedad Dramática Areyto (Areyto Dramatic Society) after the name given to the dramatic tribal dance of Puerto Rico's native people, the company emphasized the need to create Puerto Rican characters, situations, and landscapes for the stage. *Mi señoría* fit the bill perfectly and Areyto produced it. The play, which was among the company's first productions, was a great success. Rechani continued to write celebrated plays, including *Todos los ruiseñores cantan* (1964; All the Nightingales Sing), *¿Cómo se llama esta flor?* (1965; What's This Flower's Name?), *Tres piraguas en un día de calor* (1970; Three Snow Cones on a Hot Day), *Llora en el atardecer la fuente* (1971; At Sunset the Fountain Weeps), *¡Oh, dorada ilusión de alas abiertas!* (1978; Oh, Golden Illusion of Open Wings!), and *El extraño caso del señor Oblomós* (1981; The Strange Case of Mr. Oblomos)—collected with *Mi señoría* in *Teatro de Luis Rechani Agrait* (Instituto de Cultura Puertorriqueña, 1991). Rechani scholar Nilda González offers this critical assessment: "To think about Rechani's theater is to immediately recall the laughter provoked by his characters and the situations they create; it is to think of Buenaventura Padilla saying nonsense to his fellow party members."

William Carlos Williams (1883–1963) is widely recognized as one of the greatest American poets of the twentieth century and as an influential founder of literary modernism. In addition to poetry, he authored works of fiction, criticism, drama, and translation. His importance to the development of modern American poetry grew out of his commitment to recording the local experience of Rutherford, New Jersey, and its environs, where he was born and raised and where he later settled and practiced medicine as a pediatrician and obstetrician. Among his most celebrated books are *Al Que Quiere!* (Four Seas, 1917), *Spring and All* (Contact, 1923; cited by the Library of Congress as one of the eighty-eight "Books That Shaped America"), *In the American Grain* (Albert and Charles Boni, 1925), *Paterson* (Books I–V; New Directions, 1946–58), and *Pictures from Brueghel and Other Poems* (New Directions, 1962), for which he posthumously received the Pulitzer Prize for Poetry. He translated poetry and fiction from both Spanish and French, as well as poetry from classical Greek and classical Chinese. His lost translation from Spanish of

Lope de Vega's Golden Age verse play *El Nuevo Mundo descubierto por Cristóbal Colón* (*The New World Discovered by Christopher Columbus*) was made around 1914. His translation of *Mi señoría* showcases the dramatist in him. He translated it during the period he was working on *Many Loves*, his most successful play, which ran for nearly a year at the off-Broadway Living Theatre in 1959. His collected dramatic works appear in *Many Loves and Other Plays* (New Directions, 1961), which includes four full-length playscripts and the libretto of his opera on George Washington. All told, during his lifetime Williams published some twenty books of poetry and seventeen of prose, and he delivered more than three thousand babies.

Jonathan Cohen (1949–) is an award-winning poet, translator of Latin American poetry, essayist, and scholar of inter-American literature. He is the compiler/editor of William Carlos Williams's *By Word of Mouth: Poems from the Spanish, 1916–1959* (2011) and editor of the centennial edition of Williams's *Al Que Quiere!* (2017), both published by New Directions. His edition of Williams's translation of the Spanish Golden Age novella *The Dog and the Fever* (2018) was published by Wesleyan University Press. Cohen's own translations include Enrique Lihn's *The Dark Room and Other Poems* (New Directions, 1978); Ernesto Cardenal's *With Walker in Nicaragua and Other Early Poems, 1949–1954* (Wesleyan University Press, 1984), *From Nicaragua, with Love: Poems (1979–1986)* (City Lights, 1986; winner of the Robert Payne Award of the Translation Center at Columbia University), and *Pluriverse: New and Selected Poems* (New Directions, 2009); Roque Dalton's *Small Hours of the Night* (Curbstone Press, 1996; winner of the Outstanding Translation-of-the-Year Award from the American Literary Translators Association, 1997); and Pedro Mir's *Countersong to Walt Whitman and Other Poems* (Azul Editions, 1993; reprinted, Peepal Tree Press, 2018), *Two Elegies of Hope* (Spuyten Duyvil, 2019), and *Poems of Good Love . . . and Sometimes Fantasy* (Peepal Tree Press, 2023). His scholarly works include *A Pan-American Life: Selected Poetry and Prose of Muna Lee* (University of Wisconsin Press, 2004) and *Neruda in*

English: A Critical History of the Verse Translations and Their Impact on American Poetry (Stony Brook University, 1980). Cohen's poems, translations, and essays have appeared in numerous journals and other periodicals, including *American Poetry Review, The Nation, The New York Times, MultiCultural Review, The Literary Review, Literary Imagination, The American Voice, The Hudson Review, The Massachusetts Review, New Directions in Prose and Poetry, Words Without Borders, Asymptote, Review: Literature and Arts of the Americas, Translation Review, Street Magazine,* and *City Lights Review,* among others. He is a recipient of grant awards from the New York Foundation for the Arts, New York State Council on the Arts, National Endowment for the Humanities, and National Endowment for the Arts. He holds a PhD in English from Stony Brook University and an MFA in creative writing from Columbia University. For more information about Cohen's work, see jonathancohenweb.com.

Julio Marzán (1946–) is an award-winning poet, novelist, translator, essayist, and scholar. He is the author of the landmark critical work *The Spanish American Roots of William Carlos Williams* (University of Texas Press, 1994; selected as a *Choice* Outstanding Academic Title). His poetry books include *Translations Without Originals* (I. Reed Books, 1986), *Puerta de tierra* (Editorial de la Universidad de Puerto Rico, 1998; Port of Call), and *The Glue Trap and Other Poems* (Fernwood Press, 2023). From 2007 to 2010 he served as Poet Laureate of Queens, NY. His novels include *The Bonjour Gene: A Novel* (University of Wisconsin Press, 2005) and *Don't Let Me Die in Disneyland: The 3-D Life of Eddie Loperena* (Open Books, 2018), both published under J. A. Marzán to preclude any expectations of the subjects or style. Other works include *Inventing a Word: An Anthology of Twentieth-Century Puerto Rican Poetry* (Columbia University Press, 1980), *The Numinous Site: The Poetry of Luis Palés Matos* (Farleigh Dickinson University Press, 1995), *Luna, Luna: Creative Writing Ideas from Spanish, Latin American, and Latino Literature* (Teachers & Writers Collaborative, 1997), the translation of Luis Palés Matos's *Selected Poems* (Arte Público Press, 2000), and the essay collection *The Lab-*

yrinth of Multitude and Other Reality Checks on Being Latino/x (Vernon Press, 2023). His poems and essays have appeared in numerous journals, including *Parnassus, The Massachusetts Review, Tin House, New Letters, Harper's Magazine, Black Renaissance/Renaissance Noire, The Bilingual Review / La Revista Bilingüe, Review: Literature and Arts of the Americas,* and *Callaloo,* among others. By special request of editor Jonathan Cohen, he contributed the foreword to Williams's *By Word of Mouth: Poems from the Spanish, 1916–1959* (New Directions, 2011), titled "William Carlos Williams, Translator." He holds a PhD in Spanish and Portuguese languages and literatures from New York University and an MFA in creative writing from Columbia University. For more information about Marzán's work, see juliomarzan.net.

José Luis Ramos Escobar (1950–) is an award-winning Puerto Rican writer and playwright, as well as the director of several plays and the writer of television scripts. He previously served as Dean of Humanities at the University of Puerto Rico, Río Piedras, where he was a professor in the Department of Drama until 2022. He has published the novels *Sintigo* (Ediciones Huracán, 1985; Without Ya), *Matador de brújulas* (Editorial de la Universidad de Puerto Rico, 2006; Compass Killer), and *El irresistible mundo de Benedicto* (Editorial Cultural, 2010; Benedicto's Irresistible World); a short-story collection, *En la otra orilla* (Instituto de Cultura Puertorriqueña, 1992; On the Other Shore); and more than thirty plays, including *Mascarada* (1985; Masquerade; winner of the Prize of the Ateneo Puertorriqueño, 1985), *Indocumentados* (1991; Illegal Aliens), *Mano dura* (1994; Hardball), *Gení y el Zepelín* (1995; Geni and the Zepelin; winner of the International Theater Contest, University of Seville, 1993), *El olor del popcorn* (1996; produced in English as *The Smell of Popcorn,* 1998 and 2010), *El salvador del puerto* (1996; The Port Savior; winner of competition, Badajoz International Theater Festival, 1995), *Salsa gorda* (2001; Heavy Salsa; winner of the Best Production of the Year Award, 2003), and *¡Puertorriqueños?* (2001; Puerto Ricans?!; winner of the National Drama Award, 1999). Ramos has directed over twenty productions and has written several scripts for television, including *De sol a sol* (From Dawn to Dusk), a documentary about Manuel Gregorio Tavárez (for San Juan's Channel 40); *Cuando despierta el amor* (When Love Awakens), a dramatic TV series; *Sentimientos encontrados* (Mixed Emotions), a miniseries; and *Desandando la vida* (Retracing Life), a single-episode drama (all for San Juan's Channel 6). He has published several articles about the history of theater and playwriting. Ramos holds a PhD in comparative literature from Brown University.

Swan Isle Press is a not-for-profit publisher of literature
in translation including fiction, nonfiction, and poetry.

For information on books of related interest
or for a catalog of Swan Isle Press titles:
www.swanislepress.com

My Excellency
Book and cover design by Marianne Jankowski
Typeset in Adobe Jensen Pro and Doublebass.